GREAT NORTHE

GREAT NORTHERN WRITERS

Written and Researched by J. Keith Proud

Series Editor: Malcolm Parker

Published by Discovery Guides Limited,
1 Market Place, Middleton-in-Teesdale,
Teesdale, DL12 0QG. Tel: (0833) 40638

Printed by Discovery Design & Print Limited,
Cockfield, near Bishop Auckland,
Co. Durham, DL13 5BJ. Tel: (0388) 718866/7

ISBN 0 86309 011 7 © **DISCOVERY GUIDES LIMITED 1983**

All rights reserved. No part of this publication may be reproduced, stored in a retrieval system or transmitted in any form or by any means without the prior written permission of the Copyright Owner.

Contents List of the Great Northern Writers

- 6 Mark Akenside
  Alcuin
  Robert Anderson
- 7 Wystan Hugh Auden
  Barnabe Barnes
- 8 Bernard Barton
  The Venerable Bede
- 9 Gertrude M.L. Bell
- 10 Susanna Blamire
  Gordon Bottomly
  Richard Braithwaite
  Anne Brontë
- 11 Charlotte Brontë
- 12 Emily Brontë
  John Brown
  Elizabeth Barrett Browning
- 13 Thomas Burnett
  Lord Byron
- 14 Caedmon
  Joseph Storer Clouston
  Samuel Taylor Coleridge
- 15 Sara Coleridge
  Mandell Creighton
- 16 Cynewulf
  David Daiches
  Charles Lutwidge Dodgson
- 17 John Earle
  Sir Anthony S. Eddington
  Ralph Erskine
  Edward Fairfax
- 18 Hugh I'Anson Fausset
  John Forster
  Sir Samuel Garth
  Wildrid Wilson Gibson
- 19 Gerald Gould
  Thomas J. Hogg
  Constance Holme
- 20 Winifred Holtby
  Ernest William Hornung
- 21 John Horsley
  Naomi E. Jacob
  Margaret S. Jameson
- 22 Douglas Jerrold
  John Langhorne
  William Langhorne
  Henry George Liddell
- 23 Eliza Linton
  Sir Compton Mackenzie
  Wilfrid Meynell
- 24 Thomas Morton
  Norman C. Nicholson
  Anonymous
  Mark Pattison
- 25 Howard Pease
  Anna Maria Porter
  Jane Porter
- 26 Helen Beatrix Potter
  Arthur Michell Ransome
- 27 Sir Herbert E. Read
  Sir Thomas W. Reid
- 28 Joseph Ritson
  John Ruskin
  Hugh Stowell Scott
- 29 Michael Scott
  Ernest T. Seton
  Dame Edith Sitwell
- 30 Sacheverall Sitwell
  Robert Southey
- 31 James Spedding
  Laurence Sterne
- 32 Mary Stewart
  William Stubbs
- 33 Robert Smith Surtees
  Sir Henry Taylor
- 34 Thomas Tickell
  Hugh R. Trevor-Roper
  Graham Wallas
- 35 Richard Watson
  Joe Wilson
- 36 Christopher Wordsworth
- 37 William Wordsworth
  Emily Hilda Young

Extracts and Works of the Great Northern Writers

40	She Walks in Beauty (Lord Byron)
	No More a'Roving (Lord Byron)
	A Sonnet from 'The Portuguese' (Elizabeth Barrett Browning)
41	The Children's Cry (Elizabeth Barrett Browning)
42	Extract from 'The Sweetness of England' (Elizabeth Barrett Browning)
43	A Musical Instrument (Elizabeth Barrett Browning)
	Extract from 'The Ruined Cottage' (Robert Southey)
44	Extracts from the Journal of Dorothy Wordsworth
45	Extract from the 'Grasmere Journal' (Dorothy Wordsworth)
49	Extract from the Journal of Dorothy Wordsworth
50	The Daffodils (William Wordsworth)
	Peace by Ullswater (William Wordsworth)
51	Fidelity (William Wordsworth)
52	Storm over Langdale (William Wordsworth)
	Lines Written in Early Spring (William Wordsworth)
53	Extract from 'The Harbours of England' (John Ruskin)
54	Extract from 'The Lay of The Last Minstrel' (Sir Walter Scott)
57	Extracts from the Journal of Gertrude Bell
58	Introduction to the Poems of Emily Brontë (Charlotte Brontë)
60	A Poem by Emily Brontë
61	The Old Stoic (Emily Brontë)
62	Extract from 'Wuthering Heights' (Emily Brontë)
	No Coward Soul (Emily Brontë)
63	In Memory of a Happy Day in February (Anne Brontë)
64	Extract from 'Villette' (Charlotte Brontë)
65	March of the Sunday Schools (Charlotte Brontë)
69	The Months (Sara Coleridge)
70	Kubla Khan (Samuel Taylor Coleridge)
71	Answer to a Child's Question (Samuel Taylor Coleridge)
	Town and Country (Samuel Taylor Coleridge)
72	Flannan Isle (Wilfred Wilson Gibson)
74	Weel May the Keel Row (Anonymous)
75	Extract from 'Nature' (Mark Akenside)
76	Darlington Fifty Years Ago (John Horsley)
77	Wor Geordy's Album (Joe Wilson)
78	The Epitaph (Richard Watson)
79	The King's England (Caedmon)

Introduction

When we consider the great literary names which are associated with Northern England, there are some like Wordsworth, Bronte, Lewis Carroll and Beatrix Potter which spring readily to mind along with frequent visitors to the region like Sir Walter Scott, or those who married here, like Byron. But England's Northern Counties were the birthplace of many great writers who are not usually associated with their homes here; Dame Edith Sitwell was born in Scarborough and Wystan Hugh Auden is from York. Neither Lewis Carroll nor Beatrix Potter was born in the North but both saw their literary genius flower while they lived here and thus earn a place in this volume.

There are many names and facts in the book which will interest and, quite probably, surprise the reader. There is more information available about some authors than others, but we have tried to make the list of writers as comprehensive as possible. Here you will find poets, essayists, novelists, historians, journalists and dabblers, but all have earned their place in this book about northern writers.

The writers appear in alphabetical order and, where a pseudonym was used, the fact is mentioned under the entry for the author's actual name.

We have tried, where possible, to include examples of the writers' work and to offer a brief biography.

This book is only one of a series about great northern people, places, and events, so do look out for other titles.

Akenside, Mark   1721-1770

Born at Newcastle-upon-Tyne, this man was a physician as well as a poet. He was the son of a butcher, and at the age of seven, after an accident in his father's shop, he became lame for life. It was decided that he should become a minister in the Presbyterian Church and at the age of eighteen he was accordingly sent to study at Edinburgh University. He soon realised, however, that he had embarked on the wrong profession for him and decided, instead, to study medicine which he did first at Edinburgh and then at Leyden, a university town in the Netherlands where he gained his degree in 1744.

He published one of his most important poems in the same year. It was entitled "The Pleasures of Imagination" and had taken five years to write, Akenside having begun work on it when he was eighteen. The poem was well-liked and was, in fact, translated into several languages. Unfortunately, Akenside did not have such a successful start in medicine. He went into practice at Northampton but soon moved to Hampstead and then quickly to London. He was fortunate in having a wealthy friend, Jeremiah Dyson, whom he had met at Leyden. From him, he received £300 a year, which was more than useful. As a doctor, he was apparently very high-handed which fault was parodied by Tobias Smollett, another failed doctor, in his "Peregrine Pickle" of 1751. Despite this humiliation, in 1761, Akenside was created one of the physicians to Queen Charlotte, wife of George 111, which position he held until his death in 1770. Two years later his collected poems were published.

Alcuin   735 - 804

Alcuin, whose name was also spelled Ealwine, Albinus or Ealhwine, was born at York and received his education at the cloister school there. When he was forty-three, he became 'Master of the school' but soon went off on a journey to Rome; on his return in 781 he met the Holy Roman Emperor Charlemagne at Parma and travelled with him to Aix-la-Chapelle where he took up a post as advisor on education and himself educated the royal family. So it was that the culture of Northumbria travelled to Europe via Alcuin before the Viking invasions almost obliterated it here. Alcuin's writings were varied and include poetry, ethics, theology, grammar, and lives of some of the saints as well as numerous letters. In 796 he became abbot of the monastery at Tours where he lived and worked until his death in 804.

Anderson, Robert   1770 - 1833

In dealing with this Cumbrian poet, care must be taken to avoid confusion with his contemporary namesake, a poetic doctor.

This Robert Anderson was born at Carlisle where he attended the Quaker school. When he was just ten years old he became an apprentice in the calico industry learning to print the fabric, and later transferring his apprenticeship to pattern drawing. Five years of his life were spent in London.

When he was still a young man of twenty-eight his first collection of poems was published and inculed was one called "Lucy Gray" which could well have given to William Wordsworth the idea for his poem also called "Lucy Gray". Seven years later, in 1805, he brought out "Cumbrian Ballads", dialect rustic poems which proved to be very popular because they were witty and painted word pictures of Cumbrian rural life at the start of the 19th century.

In 1820, he wrote his autobiography which he published in "Poetical Works".

When Anderson died in 1833, it is said that all of Cumbria mourned his passing. He is buried in Carlisle Cathedral where there is also a marble portrait of him on the wall as a memorial.

Auden, Wystan Hugh   1907 - 1973

The poet W. H. Auden was born in York, the son of a doctor. He was educated at Holt at Gresham's School from where he went on to Christ Church, Oxford and then to Germany before returning to teach in England. He published his first book, "Poems", in 1930 when he was just twenty-three, followed by "The Orators", "The Dance of Death" and "Look Stranger" between then and 1936. He became the leader of a prolific group of Left-wing poets, although he was not himself a Communist, and his writings from this period show that he was influenced by the work of T.S. Eliot.

In 1937, he went off to the Civil War in Spain where he acted as a stretcher-bearer. As a result of his experiences there he wrote "Spain", and received, in the same year, the King's Medal for poetry. In 1938 he edited the "Oxford Book of Light Verse", and married, in the same year, Erika Mann, the daughter of a German novelist. Together they moved to the United States where Auden became an American citizen. He taught at several colleges and universities and continued to write and publish. He collaborated on three verse plays with Christopher Isherwood, and was Professor of Poetry at Oxford University from 1956 to 1961.

Barnes, Barnabe   1569 - 1609

Barnes is a little-known poet whose father became Bishop of Durham. Barnabe was probably born at Stonegrave in the Vale of Pickering while his father was curate there. The young Barnes studied at Oxford and wrote a collection of madrigals and sonnets, to which he gave the title "Parthenophil and Parthenophe" in 1593. Two years later he wrote "A Divine Centurie of Spirituall Sonnets". The other work for which he is remembered is a tragedy called "The Devil's Charter".

Barton, Bernard   1784 - 1849

Barton is often referred to as the 'Quaker' poet. Born to a Quaker family in Carlisle he led an uneventful life. When he was twenty-five he took up a position as clerk at a bank in Woodbridge where he continued to work until two days before his death. Three years after joining the bank, his "Metrical Effusions" was published in 1812, and he began to correspond with Robert Southey, who was by then living near the Coleridges at Keswick, and who was created Poet Laureate in 1813. Another of Barton's correspondents was Charles Lamb. Barton was quite a prolific writer whose other works include "Poems by an Amateur" 1818, "The Convict's Appeal" 1818, "Poems" 1820, and, in 1845, "Household Verses". This last collection caused Sir Robert Peel to secure for him a pension of £300 a year. Barton's daughter Lucy published some of his letters and poems to which was prefixed an introductory biography by her husband, Edward Fitzgerald.

Bede, (Baeda), The Venerable   673 - 735

To Bede, the monk of Jarrow, there have been given many titles. He is called variously 'The Father of English History', and 'The greatest name in the ancient literature of England'.

He was born somewhere near Monkwearmouth, now part of Sunderland, in about 673 and was, as a boy, taken into the monastery at Wearmouth under the care of the abbot, Benedict Biscop, one of the greatest scholars of his day. He then moved to the 'twin' monastery at Jarrow. In 692 he became a deacon, and in 703 a priest. As well as being engaged in the everyday business of the monastery with all which that entailed, he also taught and studied. These studies included not only the usual Latin and Greek, but also Hebrew, astronomy and medicine, and his fame as a scholar spread and he attracted many who wished to learn from him. Bede was ideally situated to further his knowledge because to Monkwearmouth and Jarrow Benedict Biscop had brought a superb library of books which he had collected on his journeys to Rome. Bede was without doubt the greatest scholar of his time and was enormously industrious, producing about forty books. Twenty-five are scriptural commentaries while the rest are lives of saints and martyrs. His two greatest works are the "History of the English Church and People" which is still in print in translation in paperback form, and "De Natura Rerum". His 'History' is a valuable source of evidence about history in Britain before 731 A.D., and 'De Natura' is an encyclopedia of the sciences known in Bede's time. Some of the information for his 'History' was taken from Roman writings but much more was extracted from native chronicles, public records and documents, and verbal and written communication with his contemporaries. Bede's 'History' was translated into Anglo-Saxon by King Alfred of Wessex. As far as can be deduced, Bede did not travel far from his monastery. He was first referred to as the Venerable Bede in 836.

When he died in 735, he was buried at Jarrow, but, in 1022, the bones were moved to Durham where they lie today in a tomb at the west end of Durham Cathedral.

There are numerous stories about Bede, but the most famous relates to his last days. At Easter, 735, it became obvious that Bede was near to death, but he continued to teach and to dictate his translation of St. John's Gospel. There was still one chapter to do, on which he worked all day and into the evening. At last, the young scribe told Bede that the work was finished. Bede replied,

"You speak truth. All is finished now."
He then chanted 'Glory to God' and died.

Bell, Gertrude Margaret Lowthian 1868 - 1926

Born at Washington Old Hall, Gertrude Bell was one of the most remarkable women of her time. Her wealthy father was an ironmaster, Sir Thomas Bell, and Gertrude earned her degree at Oxford University before she was twenty, first class honours in history. In her lifetime she achieved many things. Soon after leaving Oxford, she mad a voyage round the world and learned Persian, soon publishing in translation "Poems from the Divan of Hafix". Next, in 1899, she moved on to Jerusalem where she spent the winter learning Arabic. The Alps next took her attention and she climbed some of the most difficult peaks. Having in 1905 travelled through Cilicia and Syria, she published, two years later, her account of the journey under the title "The Desert and the Sown". She had by now become a respected archaeologist, and her work in this field was reflected in three of her books, "The Thousand and One Churches", 1909, "Amurath to Amurath", 1911, and "The Palace and Mosque of Ukhaidir", 1914.

She had travelled through Syria and Palestine several times before deciding in 1913 to set off from Damascus to try to reach the heart of Arabia. After travelling for 550 miles across the desert, she reached the central town of Northern Arabia, Hail, but she was prevented from travelling south because the tribes were said to be unfriendly. She therefore travelled 450 miles north to Baghdad becoming known to the nomadic Arabs she met on her journey.

During the First World War, she was an intelligence officer in which field she worked well using her knowledge of Arabia. After the war she returned to Mesopotamia, ostensibly as the secretary to the British Commissioner but really as the go-between with the Arabs, by whom she was well-trusted. Gertrude Bell used her influence to insist that Mesopotamia should be an independent country, and the fact that the Emir Feisal became King of Iraq was very largely her doing.

In 1923, she founded the National Museum of Baghdad. When she died in 1926, she was buried in Baghdad's British cemetery.

Blamire, Susanna   1747 - 1794

"The Muse of Cumberland", as she has been called, was born at Cardew Hall, a mile from the village of Dalston which lies to the south of Carlisle. Her father was a farmer and she wrote songs in Scottish dialect and poems about rural life in Cumbria.

It was not until 1842 that her poems were collected together. Two of her most famous songs are "Ye shall walk in silk attire" and "What ails this heart o' mine".

Susanna Blamire is buried in the churchyard at Raughton Head.

Bottomly, Gordon   1874 - 1948

This poet and playwright lived a large part of his life in the Lake District. He was born in Keighley in Yorkshire where he attended the grammar school. His first book, "The Mickle Drede and other Verses" was published when he was twenty-two and was followed by several more volumes of poetry. In 1902 he turned his attention to trying to revive English verse drama in "The Crier by Night", a medium which he used again in "The Riding to Lithend" in 1909.

In 1925 he was given the Arthur Benson Medal by the Royal Society of Literature. His last two plays were "Deirdre" in 1944 and "Kate Kennedy" in 1945.

Braithwaite, Richard   1588 - 1673

He was born near Kendal and received his education at Oxford. It is thought that during the Civil War, he fought on the Royalist side. He travelled around England and recorded some of his doings and experiences in "Drunken Barnaby's Four Journeys". Other of his works are "The Golden Fleece", a collection of poems, and a satire called "The Poet's Willow".

Bronte, Anne   1820 - 1849

Although the famous Bronte sisters were actually born at Thornton which is now part of Bradford, they passed the greater part of their lives in the now famous parsonage at Haworth on the Yorkshire moors where their Irish-born father was parson. Except for a brief stay at the academy run by Miss Wooler at Roe Head, Anne Bronte had no formal education but went, aged 19, to act as governess for the Ingham family at Blake Hall. Two years later she took up a new post with the Robinsons at Thorp Green, where she remained until 1845, the year in which she wrote a novel about the life of a governess, "Agnes Grey". It was published two years later, in 1847. Some of her poetry was published in 1846 and her second novel, "The Tenant of Wildfell Hall", came out in 1848. In the same year, tragedy struck the parsonage at Haworth. In September, the only Bronte brother, Branwell, died, a hopeless drug addict, and he was followed to the grave in December by the middle sister, Emily. Anne was very ill, too, with tuberculosis, and set off for Scarborough and the sea air with Charlotte as her companion. They left Haworth on 24th May and travelled via Leeds and York to the seaside where they arrived the next day. On the 26th they went for a drive on the beach in a donkey cart. On the 27th they watched the sunset behind the castle. The 28th saw the arrival of the doctor and later that day the life of Anne Bronte came to an end. She was twenty-nine years old. She is buried in Scarborough.

Bronte, Charlotte 1816 - 1855

Charlotte was the eldest of the three famous Bronte sisters and was also born at Thornton near Bradford, although she spent most of her life at Haworth, moving there when she was five years old. Her adventures into the field of writing began at an early age when she and her sisters and brother wrote a series of miniature books about the imaginary kingdom of Angria. When Charlotte was eight, she and her sister Emily were sent to a boarding school at Cowan Bridge in Westmorland, and with them went the two other Bronte sisters, Maria and Elizabeth who both died. Charlotte and Emily came home and were taught by their father, but Charlotte, in 1831, went to a school at Roe Head, where she later returned for a time as a teacher. Next she tried being a governess before going off to Brussels with Emily to gain enough qualifications to open their own school. Eventually, they advertised their school, but received no applications.

Charlotte virtually forced Emily to have some of her poems published, and Anne joined them in a joint volume of poems by the three sisters. They had to pay for the publication and it was not a success. Charlotte was now thirty and she and her sisters all started to write novels. Her first, "The Professor", was rejected but "Jane Eyre" was published and brought her fame, which she never really enjoyed. In 1849 there appeared her "Shirley" and, in 1853, "Villette". 1854 saw her marriage against her father's wishes to his curate, Arthur Bell Nicholls, but within a year she died in 1855.

The countryside described in the novels of the Bronte girls is still as wild as it was in their day and evokes the atmosphere so vividly portrayed in their books.

Haworth parsonage is now a museum which is open to the public and contains many pieces of Bronte memorabilia including many of their writings.

Bronte, Emily   1818 - 1848

Emily's background was almost identical to that of her sister Charlotte. Of the three sisters, she is regarded as the greatest genius and was certainly the most boisterous. When she was twenty-two she went to work as a governess in Halifax but stayed only six months before going off to Brussels with Charlotte.

Just as Branwell and Charlotte had created the imaginary country of Angria, Anne and Emily invented Gondal, about which Emily wrote in some of her poems. The first selection of these was published in 1846 and a year later her masterpiece, "Wuthering Heights," appeared. More than any of the other girls' works, this paints a vivid picture of the bleak Yorkshire moors.

She died of consumption at the age of thirty.

Brown, John   1715 - 1766

This poet and playwright was born at Rothbury in Northumberland but received his education at Wigton in Cumbria where his father was curate. He attended university at Cambridge and became a clergyman himself returning to Carlisle to work. As well as composing poems, he wrote two tragedies "Barbarossa" in 1754 and "Athelstane" in 1756, in which David Garrick, the greatest actor of the day appeared.

He was eventually asked to go to St. Petersburg to advise the Russian government about education, but his doctor would not allow him to go and he was so upset that he committed suicide by cutting his own throat.

Browning, Elizabeth Barrett 1806 - 1861

She was born Elizabeth Barrett Moulton at Coxhoe Hall in County Durham, but her father changed his name to Barrett. The family soon moved to Herefordshire. Elizabeth was a highly intelligent girl who could read Greek easily at the age of eight and by the time she was fourteen, her epic "The Battle of Marathon" had been printed privately. While still in her teens, she fell from a horse while out riding and spent years on her back. When Elizabeth was twenty, her mother died and the family moved to Wimpole Street in London. Her writings were now being published regularly.

After the death of her favourite brother in a boating accident at

Torquay she took to living in a darkened room with very few visitors but as more of her poems were published she became famous and a correspondence started between her and the poet Robert Browning who had still to make his reputation. In 1846 they met and decided to run away together to marry and to escape the jealous father. They married and went first to Paris and such was her father's wrath that he never saw her again. The next moved to Pisa but settled in Florence where she continued to write, and was always more famous than her husband. She has been called the greatest English poetess and is still highly-regarded as a sonnet-writer.

She died in Florence where she is buried.

Burnet, Thomas   1635 - 1715

Thomas Burnet was a theologian who was born at Croft near Darlington, although he went off to Cambridge and later became Master of Charterhouse. He even achieved the office of Clerk of the Closet to King William 111. Burnet was a cosmogonist, a student of the theory of the origin of the universe and in 1681 he produced "The Sacred Theory of the Earth", a well-written book, but of little scientific value. Eleven years later he published another work which really brought about his downfall; this was "Archaeologiae Philosophicae" which contained some ideas which so upset his contemoraries that he was forced to give up his Clerkship of the Closet.

Byron, George Gordon Noel, 6th Lord 1788 - 1824

Lord Byron's connection with the north of England is at the unlikely setting of Seaham where he was married. The wedding between Byron and Ann Isabella Milbanke did not take place in Seaham's old Saxon church but in the drawing room of Seaham Hall which stands near the church. The church registers contain the signatures of Byron and his wife.

Born in London, Byron had a father in the Guards who died when the lad was three. Byron went to Aberdeen Grammar School but throughout his Scottish childhood he argued endlessly with his mother who taunted him mercilessly about the foot deformity with which he had been born. He succeeded to his title at the age of ten on the death of his great-uncle. His university education was at Trinity College, Cambridge where he published his first book of poetry, "Fugitive Poems". The first part of his famous "Childe Harold's Pilgrimage" came out in 1812 and rocketed him to fame in which he revelled.

His marriage in 1815 followed a public scandal in which he was involved with Lady Caroline Lamb. The marriage was disastrous even though a daughter was born. Lady Byron was granted a separation and after another scandal, supposedly involving his sister, George Byron became a social outcast and in 1816 he went to live abroad and never returned.

His work abroad is deemed to be better than when he was writing in England.

While he was living in Pisa, he was visited by Shelley, and in 1823 he became a member of the Greek revolutionary committee which was fighting to liberate Greece which was then ruled by Turkey. He died in April 1824 of rheumatic fever and his body was returned to England for burial.

Caedmon   -680

We know of only one piece of work by this earliest English poet and that is a hymn which is quoted by Bede. The story of Caedmon is that he was one of the cattle-minders at Whitby Abbey and he was sad because he could not join in the singing around the fire at night. Then, one night, he had a vision in which an angel commanded him to sing, and, after disputing with the heavenly messenger for a while, Caedmon sang in his dream. When he awoke, he found he could indeed sing. He was taken before the Abbess Hilda to whom he told his dream and then he sang the story of the Creation. Caedmon ceased to tend the cattle and became a monk at Whitby where he continued to compose poems.

Clouston, Joseph Storer   1870 - 1944

This doctor's son was born in Cumberland and had his university education at Oxford. Although he was called to the Bar he never actually practised law. His first novel, published in 1899, "The Lunatic at Large", was highly successful. He went on to write many more successful novels, several plays, and, in 1932, a "History of Orkney", where his family came from. During World War 1 he served as Sub-Commissioner for Orkney and Shetland.

Coleridge, Samuel Taylor   1772 - 1834

Coleridge, although born in Devon, is remembered today as one of the Lakeland poets, associated with William Wordsworth.

It was after he married and settled in Somerset that he met Wordsworth who was living there at the time. They collaborated to produce "Lyrical Ballads" and Coleridge was greatly influenced by Wordsworth. He married Sara Fricker in 1795 and thus became the brother-in-law of another poet, Robert Southey who had married her sister. In Somerset he did much of his best work, including "Kubla Khan", "The Ancient Mariner", and "Christabel".

In 1800, after a year in Germany and a spell in London, he moved to the Lake District and settled at Greta Hall near Keswick where he became an opium addict. In 1804 he went off to Malta and Italy. In 1809, he left his family in Southey's care at Keswick and went off to live with the Wordsworths at Grasmere, a state of affairs which did not last. He was a 'nervous wreck' hopelessly addicted to opium.

In 1824, he was elected an Associate of the Royal Society of Literature from whom he received a much-needed pension. He died ten years later and in his last years produced work of a higher standard than he had done for a long time.

Coleridge, Sara   1802 - 1852

Although she was the only daughter of Samuel Taylor Coleridge, Sara was brought up by the Southey and Wordsworth families. She was born at Greta Hall near Keswick and in 1829 married her cousin Henry Coleridge. She edited much of her father's work and is best-remembered for her own "Pretty Lessons in Verse for Good Children", published in 1834.

Creighton, Mandell   1843 - 1901

Mandell Creighton was born at Carlisle and educated first at Durham Grammar School and then at Merton College, Oxford, where he was ordained. His first living was at Embleton in Northumberland, in view of Dunstanburgh Castle. He arrived in 1875 and lived in one of the few fortified vicarages still to be seen. Its tower dates from before the Reformation.

While vicar here, Creighton wrote the first two volumes of his "History of the Papacy" which were published in 1882. He also had published a life of Sir George Grey, and it was here that he worked on the "Northumberland County History". His wife's biography of Mandell Creighton gives an interesting account of Northumbrian life in the later years of the 19th century.

In 1884, Creighton was appointed Professor of Ecclesiastical History at Cambridge and was soon asked to edit the "English Historical Review" which he did for five years from 1886 to 1891. In 1891 he became Bishop of Peterborough and in 1897 Bishop of London.

The writing field in which he excelled was history and although he failed to complete some of his great undertakings his contribution was significant.

Cynewulf   8th century A.D.

It is thought that Cynewulf was probably born in the Saxon kingdom of Northumbria, although very little is known about him. Four of the poems which can be attributed definitely to him are preserved in Exeter Cathedral and at Vercelli in Italy. The poems are assigned to his hand because his runic signature is hidden in the verse. His poem "Elene" tells how the mother of Constantine the Great found the cross on which Christ was crucified.

Daiches, David   1912

Although he was brought up in Edinburgh, David Daiches was born, the son of a clergyman, somewhere in the north of England. he attended both school and university in Edinburgh, gaining a degree in English before going on to Oxford where he became a fellow of Balliol College.

In 1936 he published "New Literary Values" which was a look at contemporary writers. From 1937 to 1943 he taught at the University of Chicago before being appointed Second Secretary to the British Embassy in Washington D.C. In 1951, after a period as Professor of English at Cornell University, he returned to England to take up a lecturing post at Cambridge University. Authors about whom he has published studies include Virginia Woolf, Robert Louis Stevenson and Robert Burns.

Dodgson, Charles Lutwidge 1832 - 1898

This writer is much better-known by his pen-name of Lewis Carroll. Although he was born at Daresbury near Warrington in Cheshire, he came to live, at the age of eleven, at Croft, near Darlington. His father was a clergyman and the family occupied the Georgian rectory beside Croft church on the south bank of the River Tees. His father was to live there until he died twenty-five years later. The young Dodgson had four brothers and seven sisters and was good at amusing other children. The rectory is now a private residence but visitors can still look into it from the road.

Dodgson was educated first at Rugby and then at Oxford where he gained double honours in Classics and Maths before being made a Fellow of Christ Church. He was ordained at the age of twenty nine but continued to work at Christ Church. In 1865, he published the story he had made up for Alice Liddell, "Alice's Adventures in Wonderland", calling the first edition "Alice's Adventures Underground". "Through the Looking Glass" followed six years later, and then there were poems, and two not very successful books about Sylvie and Bruno. Dodgson also enjoyed composing puzzles and he wrote several mathematical works, this being the subject upon which he lectured at Oxford. He was buried in Guildford.

Earle, John   1601 - 1665

He was born at York and educated at Oxford University where he was made a Fellow of Merton College. He took holy orders and was tutor to King Charles 11 as a boy, following him into exile during the Commonwealth and acting as his chaplain. Returning to England with Charles, he became firstly Dean of Westminster and then Bishop of Worcester and soon afterwards Bishop of Salisbury. He was a famous wit and an essayist of considerable note.

Eddington, Sir Arthur Stanley 1882 - 1944

Better remembered as an astronomer than as an author, Eddington was born at Kendal in Cumbria. His father was headmaster of a school there and Eddington attended both Manchester and Cambridge universities eventually becoming a fellow of Trinity College. Before being appointed Professor of Astronomy at Cambridge in 1913, he was, for seven years, chief assistant at Greenwich Royal Observatory. Although highly-respected in his academic field, he also contributed significantly to popular astronomical literature. He wrote others "Stars and Atoms", "Science and the Unseen World", and "The Expanding Universe".

Erskine, Ralph   1685 - 1752

Born at Monylaws Farm, at Monylaws in Northumberland, Ralph Erskine was to spend most of his life in Scotland. His father, a Covenanting minister, sent him to be educated in Edinburgh, a far cry from his native Cheviot Hills. He became a minister himself in Dunfermline and was one of the founders of the new 'Secession Church' in 1736. His poetry was very popular, appearing in print as "Gospel Sonnets" and "Scripture Songs".

Fairfax, Edward   1580 - 1635

Little is remembered about this author from Fuystone near Knaresborough. Son of Sir Thomas Fairfax, he led a secluded life and when only twenty he translated "Jerusalem Delivered" by Tasso. He dedicated his work to the Queen, and, being like the next monarch, James 1, interested in witchcraft, he wrote a treatise on the subject, which appeared in 1621.

Fausset, Hugh I'Anson   1895 - 1965

Born at Killington in Westmorland, Hugh Fausset was the son of a very strict clergyman whose own father had been a Biblical scholar of great renown. He attended Sedbergh School and then went on to Cambridge.

As well as composing two volumes of autobiographical poetry in 1933 and 1952 he was well-known for his critical literary studies of Keats, Tennyson, Donne, Coleridge, Tolstoy, Wordsworth and Walt Whitman, all of which were published between 1922 and 1942.

Forster, John   1812 - 1876

This biographer's father was a butcher on Newcastle's Quayside. Born in Newcastle, John Forster went to the Grammar School there and then to University College, London where he studied law. He did become a barrister at the Inner Temple but quickly realized that he preferred writing so, when still only twenty-two, he became Drama Critic of "The Examiner", becoming its editor thirteen later. In those years he also edited the "Foreign Quarterly Review" and the "Daily News". He is best known for his friendship with Charles Lamb and Leigh Hunt and for his excellent biography of Charles Dickens, but he also chronicled the lives of Oliver Goldsmith and Landor and began work on a biography of Dean Swift. He also wrote "Statesmen of the Commonwealth of England".

Garth, Sir Samuel   1661 - 1719

Some controversy surrounds the place of birth of this doctor and poet. It is claimed both by Bolam in County Durham and Bowland Forest in Yorkshire. After leaving Cambridge University he set up his medical practice in London. He was a friend of Addison, the Whig, and of the poet, Pope. As well as being appointed to the elevated position of Physician General to the Army, he was also one of King George 1's doctors and was knighted by him in 1714.

In 1699 he wrote "The Dispensary", which was a poetic satirical attack on uncharitable doctors.

When the great poet Dryden died in 1700, forgotten by practically everyone, it was Sir Samuel Garth who provided his funeral in Westminster Abbey.

Gibson, Wilfrid Wilson   1878 - 1962

A red stone pillar in Hexham market place carries on it an inscription by local poet Wilfrid Wilson Gibson. A great lover of everything to do with Nature and particularly the moors and the hills, he was born in Hexham in 1878. As a young boy he started to write poetry and was never employed in any other occupation.

It was the "Spectator" which first published some of his work in 1897. Five years later, "Mountain Lovers", a book of his poems, was published. He was desperate to join the forces when war broke out in 1914 and repeatedly fought against his rejection on the grounds of poor eyesight until, in 1917, he was finally accepted.

His poetry belongs to the Georgian school and is about everyday things; in fact he is referred to as the 'poet of the industrial poor'. If you want to read poetry about Northumbrian scenery, then Gibson is the perfect choice. Many of his volumes are still available from bookshops and libraries, and include "Urlyn the Harper", "Stonefolds", "Daily Bread", "Krindlesyke" and "Kestrel Edge".

Gould, Gerald   1885 - 1936

From seaside roots at Scarborough, Gerald Gould was educated at London's University College and then at Merton, Oxford, where he was a Fellow from 1909 to 1916. Before giving up his fellowship, he joined the journalistic staff of the 'Daily Herald' with whom he stayed until taking up an appointment with the 'Saturday Review' in 1926. He was also literary critic for several newspapers and he wrote poetry too.

His poetry began to appear in print in 1906 with "Lyrics", soon followed by "Poems" and "The Happy Tree". He also published two sets of essays and "The English Novel of Today".

Hogg, Thomas Jefferson   1792 - 1862

Born at Norton in south-east Durham, Thomas Hogg was sent to Durham School and then to University College, Oxford where he met the poet Shelley. The two young men became firm friends and literary collaborators and Hogg eventually wrote a biography of Shelley including an account of their time together at Oxford. A year after arriving at university, Shelley issued a pamphlet about "The Necessity of Atheism" for which he and Hogg left. In 1817 he completed his legal studies and was called to the Bar. He pursued a career as a barrister. It was an article called "Reminiscences of Shelley" published in 1832 which led to his being commissioned to write the poet's biography, but when the first two volumes appeared in 1858 they were considered to be so offensive that the work was not finished.

Holme, Constance   1881 - 1955

Many authors get their first toe-hold on the ladder of success by winning a literary award, and such was the case with Constance Holme. Born at Milnthorpe in Westmorland she came from a large family of fourteen children. Three years after her marriage in 1916 to Frederick Punchard, she won the Femina Vie Heureuse Prize for her novel "The Splendid Faring".

Her novels are usually set in Westmorland and include "The Lonely Plough", "The Old Road from Spain" and "The Trumpet in the Dust".

Holtby, Winifred 1898 - 1935

Many would agree that Winifred Holtby did not live long enough to realise her full potential, having died, of overwork it is said, at thirty-seven. Many readers will be familiar with her novel "South Riding", which she completed just before her death.

Born at Rudstone in Yorkshire, she was educated at Scarborough's Queen Margaret's School and then at Somerville College, Oxford. Having served during World War 1 in the Women's Auxiliary Army Corps, she went, in 1921, to London where she lived with Vera Brittain whom she knew at Oxford. Her story was told in a television series named after her novel, "Testament of Youth". In 1940, Vera Brittain wrote a tribute to Winifred Holtby called "Testament of Friendship".

In London, Winifred Holtby wrote for the weekly "Time and Tide" but also travelled Europe giving lectures for the League of Nations Union.

In 1932 she wrote an appreciation of "Virginia Woolf". Another of her best-known novels was "The Land of Green Ginger" which appeared in 1927.

Hornung, Ernest William 1866 - 1921

A crossword clue might well suggest that this Middlesbrough-born author had connections with Sherlock Holmes.

Educated at Uppingham, he moved to Australia for health reasons when he was eighteen, and he lived there until 1886. Seven years later, having written "A Bride from the Bush", a novel with an Australian setting, he married Constance, the sister of Sir Arthur Conan Doyle, creator of Sherlock Holmes. In 1899, Hornung created his own amateur detective Raffles, who first appeared as "The Amateur Cracksman". In all, he was used in four novels.

Following his journeys in France during World War 1 where he organised a mobile library, he wrote "Notes of a Camp Follower" and a book of poetry which he called "The Young Guard".

Horsley, John   1817-1893

John Horsley's fame, such as it is today, rests mainly on the fact that he may well have designed the first Christmas card, a claim now supported by a wide body of opinion. He was also, however, a writer of some note in his time.

He was born in Newcastle, but was a resident of Darlington for more than fifty years where he composed many poems. Two readers who thought highly of him were Queen Victoria and Mr. Gladstone. His verses were published collectively in two volumes, 'Stray Leaves by the Banks of the Tees', and 'The Royal Rose'. He was a lover of Nature, not only here in England but also in Holland, Germany, Belgium and Ireland where he also wrote.

He was also a great worker in the cause of Temperance and a keen advocate of the Sunday School movement. He taught in Sunday schools for over fifty years and was Vice-President of the Darlington Sunday School Union for twenty years. As well as being a poet, he was a great essay-writer on such varied topics as Juvenile Crime, Science and History, and Poets and Poetry.

He was an accurate observer, as can be seen from his poem in this volume, 'Darlington Fifty Years Ago' about the town before the birth of the railways.

Jacob, Naomi Ellington   1884 - 1964

Born in Ripon and educated at Middlesbrough High School, Naomi Jacob started work as a pupil-teacher at the age of fifteen. During the First World War when she was a supervisor in an armaments factory she developed tuberculosis and had to spend three years in a sanatorium. She worked successfully on the professional stage and had her first novel, "Jacob Ussher", published in 1926.

By 1930, her health had deteriorated again and so she went to the more favourable climate of Italy where she lived beside Lake Garda until the outbreak of war in 1939. During the war she served with E.N.S.A. and continued to write her novels. Her biography of Marie Lloyd came out in 1936 and her series of autobiographies all entitled "Me", were published between 1933 and 1954, the first carrying the amusing title "Me - A Chronicle About Other People".

Jameson, Margaret Storm   1897 -

Born in Whitby, this writer has been variously classified as critic, editor, publicity writer and novelist. Her University thesis after an education at Leeds and London was "Modern Drama in Europe". Her best novels reflect her family background they being a shipbuilding trilogy and she coming from a shipbuilding family.

Her only play, written in 1928, was "Full Circle" and her autobiography, "No Time Like the Present" came out in 1933.

Jerrold, Douglas   1893 - 1964

This notable historian was born in Scarborough and sent to Westminster School and subsequently Oxford University. In the First World War he was with the Royal Naval Division, his experiences with which he later documented. In 1928 he wrote an account of "The War on Land 1914 - 1918". Between 1930 and 1936 he was editor of the "English Review" and in 1945 he became editor of the "New English Review". His "Introduction to the History of England" was published in 1949. His novels "The Truth About Quex" and "Storm over Europe" came out in 1927 and 1930.

Langhorne, John   1735 - 1779 and William   1721 - 1772

These two brothers were born at Winton in Westmorland, sons of a clergyman, and both were themselves to take holy orders. In 1766, John became Rector of Blagdon in Somerset having spent two years as a curate in London. He went on to become a Prebendary of Wells Cathedral. He also wrote poetry which was well-received in his day and in 1766 were published his "Poetical Works". Much of his descriptive poetry is like that written later by Wordsworth.

The great joint literary work carried out by the brothers was a translation of Plutarch's "Lives" in 1770.

Liddell, Henry George   1811 - 1898

He was born at Binchester which is between Bishop Auckland and Spennymoor. His father was curate of St. Andrew's at South Church and his mother was a niece of the Earl of Strathmore. While he was still an infant the family moved to Boldon, and at the age of six he was first taught Latin. At eight he was sent away to school near Ripon and from there on to Charterhouse. Here his fellow pupil, W.M. Thackeray, copied Latin exercises from him. His next step was to Christ Church, Oxford, where he shone as a student of Classics, and with Robert Scott, a fellow student, he began to write a Greek Lexicon, a task which took twelve years to complete. Until then, all Greek dictionaries had been translated into Latin or German.

At the age of twenty-five Liddell became a tutor at Christ Church and also became a Church of England minister. When he married, he had to leave Christ Church and became headmaster of Westminster School.

In 1854 he returned to Christ Church as Dean and subsequently accepted the post of Vice-Chancellor of Oxford University. At the age of eighty he retired, but all through his working life he constantly revised his Lexicon.

His daughter, Alice, gained a more lasting fame than he. One of her father's friends was Charles Lutwidge Dodgson, better known now as Lewis Carroll and he wrote "Alice in Wonderland" for Alice Liddell and used her as the heroine.

Linton, Eliza   1822 - 1898

This little-known novelist was born at Keswick, the daughter of a clergyman, but at the age of twenty-three she moved to London where in 1846 her first book "Azeth, the Egyptian" was published but met, like her two subsequent novels, with very little success. She became a journalist with the "Morning Chronicle" and in 1858 married poet and wood-engraver, W.J. Linton but they separated in 1867. Mrs. Linton's next novels made her very popular and included "The True History of Joshua Davidson" 1872, and "Christopher Kirkland" 1885.

Mackenzie, Sir Compton   1883 - 1972

Born Edward Montague Compton, this fine novelist was born at West Hartlepool. Both of his parents had theatrical backgrounds and his sister was the actress Fay Compton. His father was the actor Edward Compton and his mother Virginia Bateman. Mackenzie adhered to the family theatrical tradition by joining the Oxford University Dramatic Society while he was at Magdalen College, Oxford. His studies were towards a career in the legal profession but he began to write and in 1907 published a play, "The Gentleman in Grey". In 1911, his first novel, "The Passionate Elopement," was very successful, but he made his name with his second, "Carnival," which came out in 1912; it was about life in the theatre. One of his best novels was "Sinister Street", published in 1913.

During the First World War he seved in the Dardanelles and recalled his experiences there many years later in 1928 in "Gallipoli Memories". Later in the war he was attached to the Secret Service which led to "Extremes Meet", again in 1928.

In 1919, after being awarded the O.B.E., he went to live in the Outer Hebrides on the Island of Barra. As well as being one of the founders of the Scottish Nationalist Party, he was made Lord Rector of Glasgow University in 1931. It was the Scottish island life which led him to write, in 1947, "Whisky Galore" of which a highly successful film was made.

He became Sir Compton Mackenzie in 1952.

Meynell, Wilfrid   1852 - 1948

Wilfrid Meynell was given a Quaker education in Croydon and

York, although he was born in Newcastle where his father was the owner of a colliery.

He went to London in 1870 to pursue a career in journalism and by 1881 was editor of the "Weekly Register". He used the pen-name John Oldcastle when he published his first book "Journals and Journalism".

In 1934 he was given the C.B.E. for his work which included "The Man Disraeli" and "Aunt Sarah and the War".

Morton, Thomas   1764 - 1838

Born in Durham City, Thomas Morton was destined for a career in law but he left Lincoln's Inn to take up play-writing and wrote twenty-five in his lifetime. In 1796 appeared his "The Way to get Married" which was followed in 1798 by "Speed the Plough". For most of his life he lived at Pangbourn near Reading but moved to London in 1828.

His son, John, was a famous writer of farces.

Nicholson, Norman Cornthwaite   1914

Probably most famous for his play "The Old Man of the Mountains" in which the prophet Elijah appears set in the Lake District, Norman Nicholson was born at Millom in Cumberland. His first poetry book, "Five Rivers", came out in 1944. He also wrote other plays and several novels along with critical studies of Cowper and H.G. Wells.

Onymous, A.N.

All schoolchildren are familiar with this prolific mediaeval writer whose dates and place of birth are, unfortunately, not recorded. It is certain, however, that he spent some time in the north of England since from his pen came 'Chevy Chase' and 'The Battle of Otterburn' as well as many other northern tales.

He must be included in any list of Great Northern Writers not only for his skill as a poet and story-teller, but because he has been denied, for centuries, the credit he so richly deserves.

Pattison, Mark   1813 - 1884

Although he was born at Hornby in Yorkshire, Mark Pattison soon moved to his clergyman father's new parish of Hauxwell, a dales village. At Oxford, after being educated at home, he entered Oriel College and then became a fellow of Lincoln College in 1839. A very shy man, he almost became a Roman Catholic, and wrote two "Lives of The Saints", but, instead, he became a very influential tutor. This period of his life came to an end when he failed to get himself elected Master of his college, and he withdrew even further into himself and buried himself in his studies. In 1858, he served for three months as Berlin correspondent for "The Times".

He wrote for several magazines and became highly thought-of, particularly after his study of elementary education in Germany was published in 1859.

In 1861, he was elected rector of Lincoln College and married a year later. He was a great student of the works of John Milton of whom he wrote a biography as well as editing a collection of his sonnets.

He died at Harrogate.

Pease, Howard   1863 - 1928

In the corner of Otterburn churchyard there stands a tall Celtic cross to mark the grave of this Northumberland author who does not even receive a mention in literary biographical dictionaries. Howard Pease wrote several novels and many short stories and was a masterful storyteller who perfectly caught the Northumbrian character and temperament.

For more than twenty years he lived in Otterburn Tower, a house with battlements, just off Otterburn main street.

His greatest work was "Northumbria's Decameron", a history of the county which was left unfinished by Mandell Creighton.

Pease's characters range from the gentry to miners and from vicars to rogues and his now-neglected stories are a joy to read.

Porter, Anna Maria   1780 - 1832

The lesser-known of the two Porter sisters, Anna Maria was born in Durham but educated at Edinburgh where at the age of thirteen she started to write her "Artless Tales". These were published when she was still only fifteen. At seventeen her novel "Walsh Volville" was brought out, to be followed a year later by another, "Octavia".

Her best-known novel, about the French Revolution, "The Hungarian Brothers", was published in 1807.

A volume of her poems, "Ballad Romances" was well received in 1811.

Other novels from her pen were "Don Sebastian", "The Knight of Saint John", "The Recluse of Norway" and, her last, "Barony".

Porter, Jane   1776 - 1850

Like her younger sister Anna Maria, Jane Porter was born in

Durham but was educated in Edinburgh. Her father was a surgeon in the army and one of the family friends was Sir Walter Scott.

Having moved to London, in 1803 she wrote a book, "Thaddeus of Warsaw", which ran to twelve editions, and she followed it in 1810 with a novel based on the life of the Scottish hero William Wallace. Called "The Scottish Chiefs" it proved very popular in Scotland and was even translated into German and Russian, despite the fact that the critics thought Wallace, as depicted in the book, a stilted character.

Her other successful novels were "Tales Round a Winter's Hearth", "The Pastor's Fireside" and "The Field of Forty Footsteps".

Potter, Helen Beatrix 1866 - 1943

Although she was born in Kensington at the height of the Victorian era, Beatrix Potter is closely associated with a very different area, the Lake District where she lived much of her life. She never went to school but had a governess, and every year the wealthy Potter family spent several months holidaying in the country. One of their favourite summer retreats was a large house, Wray Castle, on the edge of Lake Windermere. Beatrix Potter was a solitary child who loved to draw and paint. She drew from life or went to the Victoria and Albert Museum to copy their specimens. She did illustrate books for other people like Frederick Weatherley in the 1980's and Clifton Bingham in 1896.

Her own writing began unintentionally as letters to children, both Peter Rabbit and Squirrel Nutkin coming to life in this way.

So well did she love the Lake District that in 1905 she bought Hill Top Farm in the village of Near Sawrey beside Hawkshead. Frederick Warne was by then publishing the small books for which she is best remembered and she used many sites in and around Sawrey for illustrations in her books. Anyone familiar with her books will, on a visit to Hill Top, instantly recognise many of the settings. The house, now a museum, is kept much as it was when Tabatha Twitchit lived there and became involved in the adventure with the Roly Poly Pudding.

In 1913, when she was forty-seven, she married an Ambleside solicitor, William Heelis and went to live at Castle Cottage, a larger house near Hill Top, but she kept her little farmhouse and went there when she wanted to work or to be alone.

After her marriage, her output of books decreased considerably. On her death in 1943, she left more than four thousand acres of the Lake District to the National Trust.

Ransome, Arthur Michell 1884 - 1967

A Leeds man by birth, Arthur Ransome qualifies for entry in this volume mainly because of his association with the Lake District, Lake Windermere in particular.

The young Ransome, whose father was History Professor at Leeds

University, was educated at Rugby School. When he left, he found a position in the office of a London publisher and soon turned to writing himself. In 1910 he published a critical study of Edgar Allan Poe, followed two years later by one of Oscar Wilde.

Next he went to Russia before the outbreak of the First World War, and when he returned, having studied the language, he wrote "Six Weeks in Russia". In 1921 came "Crisis in Russia".

His fame rests, however, in his brilliant children's books which in no way "talk down" to young readers. The first of the long series was "Swallows and Amazons" in 1931, subsequently made into a lovely film. The other titles deserve a mention and are "Peter Duck", "Winter Holiday", "Pigeon Post", "We didn't mean to go to Sea", "Secret Water", "The Big Six", "The Picts and the Martyrs" and "Great Northern".

His C.B.E. was conferred in 1953.

Read, Sir Herbert Edward
1893 - 1968

Although Herbert Read of Kirbymoorside in Yorkshire went to university at Leeds, his studies were interrupted by the outbreak of the First World War. Serving as a captain in the Yorkshire Regiment, he was awarded the D.S.O. and the M.C., and after being demobbed he worked in the Treasury Department and then in the Victoria and Albert Museum where he stayed for nine years. Next came two years as Professor of Fine Arts at Edinburgh and then from 1933 to 1939 he was editor of the "Burlington Magazine".

In the literary field, Read is remembered as a great exponent of free verse and as a critic.

Several volumes of his poems have been published since 1919, as well as many books of criticism.

Reid, Sir Thomas Wemyss
1842 - 1905

It is amazing how many writers were the children of clergymen, which was again the case with Thomas Reid whose father was a Congregationalist minister. For seventeen years from 1870 he edited the "Leeds Mercury", after which he moved to the editorship of "The Speaker" in London where he worked from 1890 to 1899. He also worked as manager of the publishers, Cassell.

He wrote a biography of Charlotte Bronte and several novels.

Ritson, Joseph   1752 - 1803

Born in Stockton-on-Tees, Joseph Ritson moved to London as a young man of twenty-three. There he worked as a conveyancer but also indulged in antiquarian pursuits, in particular the study of early English poetry, examples of which he collected assiduously.

Unfortunately, he had a violent temper which led him into many quarrels, notably with Dr. Johnson. His spelling was so peculiar that he was ridiculed for it as well as for the fact that he was a vegetarian. In his criticism of the works of others he was fierce. He had several collections of ancient poetry published including many of the Robin Hood ballads in 1795.

Tragically, he died completely insane.

Ruskin, John   1819 - 1900

This Victorian writer was born in London. His father was a Scottish wine merchant. The young Ruskin attended Christ Church, Oxford where he took his degree in 1842. He studied painting and in 1843 he published the first volume of "Modern Painters". He also interested himself in architecture and between 1849 and 1853 wrote two books on the subject, "The Seven Lamps of Architecture" and "The Stones of Venice". He illustrated the books himself and was a great supporter of the Pre-Raphaelite movement and wrote pamphlets in support of it. In 1851 he wrote his famous fairy story "The King of the Golden River". His interests were wide reaching, wood and metal engraving, sculpture, geology and religion. His "Time and Tide" is a collection of letters to a working man in Sunderland. His poems often appear illustrated with his own work. Between 1869 and 1879 Ruskin was Slade professor of Art at Oxford.

His connection with the north is that in later years he lived at Brantwood, a house overlooking Lake Coniston and it was there that he died. He actually bought the property after his mother died in 1871. He was a generous man but often intolerant and irritable.

Scott, Hugh Stowell   1862 - 1903

Henry Seton Merriman is the name under which this author wrote his books. He was born at Newcastle, the son of a ship-owner but was educated abroad at Loretto and Wiesbaden. His occupation was as a clerk in an insurance office but in 1888 his first novel was published. It was followed four years later by his first best-seller, "The Slave of the Lamp".

His historical novels have been compared with the work of Alexander Dumas, and he wrote a string of successful novels from 1894 to his death.

Some of his books were "The Grey Lady", "The Sowers", and "In Kedar's Tents".

Scott, Michael   1175 - 1234

Mystery surrounds even the dates of birth and death of this man who was born somewhere on the Scottish border. Known as the Wondrous Wizard, he was a translator, astrologer and tutor. He was educated at Oxford and in Paris and emerged as one of the greatest scholars of his time. He read Arabic fluently and translated some of Aristotle's work in Arabic into Latin. He worked at Palermo as tutor and court astrologer to Frederick 11. He lived at Toledo in Spain from 1209 to 1220 after which he returned to Palermo where he was offered but seemingly refused the archbishopric of Cashel in 1223.

Throughout Europe, he was famed as a magician and he is referred to in Dante's "Inferno". Some claim that he was not from the Scottish border but an Irishman, but the historian Camden says that he was a Cistercian monk from Holme Cultram in Cumberland.

His supposed grave is in Melrose Abbey and he has passed into Border folk-lore as having split the Eildon Hills into three sections using his powerful magic.

Sir Walter Scott writes of his power as a magician in "The Lay of the Last Minstrel".

Seton, Ernest Thompson   1860 - 1946

Far better-known in Canada than in his native England, Ernest Seton Thompson, as he was christened, was born at South Shields in Co. Durham. At the age of six, he went to live with his family in a remote part of Canada where he was brought up until being sent to attend the Toronto Collegiate Institute. Later he was a student at the Royal Academy in London.

In 1910, he wrote "Scouting for Boys" and was one of the founders of the Scout movement in America.

His fame rests, however, on his books about wild animals which he also illustrated. There are many of them ranging from "Wild Animals I Have Known" in 1898 to "The Trail of an Artist-Naturalist", an autobiography published in 1940.

Sitwell, Dame Edith   1887 - 1964

One of the north's most famous poets and critics, Edith Sitwell was born at Scarborough. Many were amused by her habit of wearing medieval fashions. Her brothers shared her literary interests and in 1916 they combined to publish "Wheels".

As a critic, she produced many volumes, including an excellent study of Alexander Pope in 1930, and a survey of "English Eccentrics" in 1932.

Her books of poetry are many and include "Facade" in 1950 and "Gardeners and Astronomers" in 1952. The Royal Society of London awarded her a medal in 1933, and in 1954, the year, incidentally, in which she was converted to Roman Catholocism, she became a Dame Grand Cross of the British Empire. Oxford, Durham and Leeds universities all awarded her honorary doctorates.

In 1963 she became a Companion of Literature in the Royal Society of Literature.

Sitwell, Sacheverall   1897 - 1969

This, the brother of Dame Edith, was also born at Scarborough, but was sent away to Eton and Oxford for his education. After the First World War, during which he served with the Grenadier Guards, he became an art and music critic as well as a poet. His musical studies include Mozart and Liszt and he wrote at length about various aspects of Baroque art.

He was Sheriff of Northamptonshire in 1948 and 1949.

Southey, Robert   1774 - 1843

Although born in Bristol, Robert Southey is always linked with the north because of his associations with Wordsworth and Coleridge and because he lived at Greta Hall, Keswick in the Lake District. His father, a linen draper, was not a success in business and it was left to his uncle to send him to Westminster School where he went in 1788. He was expelled five years later, however, for writing an article, condemning flogging, for the school magazine.

It was decided he should go into the Church, so he went up to Balliol College, Oxford where he formed a friendship with Coleridge whose brother-in-law he became in 1795, when he married Edith Fricker, Coleridge marrying Sara Fricker, her sister.

Southey forsook the idea of the Church and tried his hand at medicine and lecturing at neither of which he met with much success. He went to visit an uncle in Portugal and while there and in Spain he gained an excellent knowledge of the customs and literature of Iberia.

On his return to England he diversified yet again and tried to take up the law but was a dismal failure.

In 1803, he and his wife went to live at Greta Hall where the Coleridges were already in residence, but a year later Coleridge set off on his travels leaving Southey to look after his family. Several friends helped him financially, and, in 1807, he was given a government pension.

His biographies include among their subjects Admiral Lord Nelson, John Bunyan and Wesley, and he wrote a "History of the Peninsular War" as well as a "Naval History".

To most readers, the most interesting fact about Robert Southey is that he wrote the classic nursery tale, "The Three Bears" in his book, "The Doctor", and others will know his "Battle of Blenheim".

In 1813 he became Poet Laureate and was offered but rejected a baronetcy.

His second wife, Caroline Ann Bowles, had known him for many years, and was also a writer. They married in 1839 when he was failing badly, both mentally and physically, and she nursed him through the last four years of his life.

Spedding, James   1808 - 1881

He was born at Mirehouse near Bassenthwaite in Cumberland. In the old church at Bassenthwaite are memorials to other members of the Spedding families, but the marble memorial to James Spedding lies in the church of Holy Trinity in Whitehaven, and it shows him with his long pigtail. Spedding was to spend thirty years studying the life and works of Francis Bacon.

Spedding was the son of a Cumberland squire and was schooled at Bury St. Edmunds before going on to Trinity College, Cambridge. He served for some years in the Colonial Office, from 1835 to 1841, and in 1842 went to America as Lord Ashburton's secretary. Had he not devoted himself so utterly to his study of Bacon he could well have had a brilliant diplomatic career.

He died tragically when in 1881 he was run over by a cab.

Sterne, Laurence   1713 - 1768

Laurence Sterne was, by all accounts, a most unpleasant human being, but a brilliant writer.

Born at Clonmel in Ireland, son of an infantry officer, he was also the grandson of an Archbishop of York. He spent some of his early life in Ireland because that was where his father was serving. Because of his father's military wanderings, the boy was entrusted to one of his relatives in England who sent him to school in Halifax when he was ten. After school he went to Jesus College, Cambridge. Having gained his degree, he went to live with his uncle, Jacques Sterne, who was an archdeacon at York.

Two years later in 1738, having taken holy orders, he became, thanks to family influence, vicar of Sutton-on-The-Forest and a prebendary of York. The York minster office came about because in 1741 he married Elizabeth Lumley whose father 'pulled strings' to help his new son-in-law and also obtained for him the neighbouring living of Stillington. There were two children of the marriage, both girls, but only one, Lydia, survived.

In 1759, Sterne had published at York the first two volumes of "The Life and Opinions of Tristram Shandy". A year later, the books were published in London and were immediately enormously popular. Sterne went to London himself to meet his public, and a second edition of the books was rushed out to be followed by a collection of sermons by "The Reverend Mr. Yorick." While all this was happening, a nobleman gave

Sterne the perpetual living of Coxwold.

This was the parish where the body of Oliver Cromwell is thought to be buried. Sterne did not spend a lot of time here but for the last eight years of his life he lived in Shandy Hall, an old gabled house with a huge chimney. While he lived here, he wrote "The Sentimental Journey" and "Journal to Eliza", and he finished "Tristram Shandy".

He has been called the greatest humorist of his age but it is unlikely that his parishioners thought him anything but eccentric.

In his later years he suffered very badly from pleurisy. He died in London. He died a debtor and a tiny cortege followed him to his grave but his body was dug up within a matter of days and dissected by a Cambridge professor. Even his estranged wife came to an unpleasant end, for, having married a Frenchman after Sterne's death, she lost her head on the guillotine.

Stewart, Mary   Born 1916

Mary Stewart is a Durham woman whose novels are always best-sellers. She attended Durham University after schooling at Penrith and Ripon. From 1941 to 1956 she was on the academic staff of Durham University.

Some of her highly successful novels include "Wildlife at Midnight", "My Brother Michael" and "The Moon-Spinners".

Stubbs, William   1825 - 1901

An interesting historian, William Stubbs was born at Knaresborough in Yorkshire where his father was a solicitor. He attended Ripon Grammar School and then, after obtaining his Oxford degree, became a Fellow of Trinity College, Oxford. Having become a clergyman, he was given the parish of Navestock in Essex in 1850. He was to remain there for sixteen years. In 1860 he was also appointed diocesan inspector of schools.

In 1858 he saw published his "Registrum Sacrum Anglicanum" a catalogue of English bishops since St. Augustine. In 1862 he accepted an appointment as librarian at Lambeth Palace and four years later became Professor of Modern History at Oxford. During his time there he published the three volumes of his "Constitutional History of England" which was a classic piece of work. In 1876 came "The Early Plantaganets".

Despite the immense volume of literary work he produced, he still managed to attain high office in the Church. In 1879 he was made a canon of St. Paul's Cathedral and, in 1884, Bishop of Chester. Five years afterwards he took over the diocese of Oxford.

Surtees, Robert Smith   1805 - 1864

This Durham novelist is remembered for his sporting novels and little is known of his early life. His father became the local squire when he bought Hamsterley Hall in 1810. Young Robert went to school at nearby Ovingham until he was thirteen and from there he moved to Durham Grammar School which he attended for a year. In 1822 he was articled to a solicitor in Newcastle and subsequently to another in London. Surtees' heart lay, however, not in the office but in the hunting field so loved by his father. He hunted with some of the London packs but did not rate them very highly, and lent his allegiance to the Southdown Foxhounds at Brighton which spa he visited throughout his life and where he eventually died. In 1829, he went on holiday to Boulogne and while there he was given a pack of hounds with which he hunted but he was summoned frequently for trespass and eventually concluded that the French were not a very sporting lot. He returned to England and began to scribble, as he put it. He was employed as a writer by the "Sporting Magazine" and was, for a year, its hunting correspondent, earning quite a large salary. He created a character called Jorrocks who was to give him immortality, but he quarralled with his employers and started a rival magazine, the "New Sporting Magazine" in 1831. During the magazine's five year life, Surtees was sued for libel for criticizing the inns in Leamington, but he was ordered to pay damages of a farthing only.

In 1836, having sold his magazine, he returned to Hamsterley where his father and mother both soon died. His elder brother having died in 1831, Robert was now the squire, and made the place his permanent home. He became, as might be expected, a magistrate, an officer in the yeomanry, and Deputy Lieutenant for County Durham, but he also kept a pack of hounds and was asked to be Master of the South Durham Hunt but declined because they hunted too far away and, anyway, he was far too busy.

His Jorrocks stories were published as novels between 1838 and 1845, the early editions being illustrated by H.K. Browne, otherwise known as Phiz. Surtees did not like his work to appear under his own name and he avoided this by using a variety of pseudonyms. In 1841, he married Elizabeth Fenwick by whom he had four children.

He continued to write until his death and even penned an unpublished work on farming in County Durham.

Taylor, Sir Henry   1800 - 1886

Taylor, born at Bishop Middleham in County Durham was the son of a gentleman farmer and was educated at home. At the age of twenty-four he became a clerk in the Colonial Office, having formerly had a short-lived stint as a midshipman in the Royal Navy.

He remained in the Colonial Service for almost fifty years and became an influential policy-maker.

He wrote plays, prose and verse, and his autobiography, published the year before he died, includes pen portraits of literary men like Wordsworth, Carlyle, Southey and Tennyson.

His plays, written between 1827 and 1862, include four tragedies and a comedy. His poetry, which was published as "The Eve of the Conquest", is lyric verse.

He was created Knight Commander of St. Michael and St. George in 1872. He died in Bournemouth.

Tickell, Thomas   1686 - 1740

Dr. Samuel Johnson was of the opinion that Tickell's poem about Addison's burial was the greatest funeral poem in the English language.

Tickell was born in the vicarage at Bridekirk near Carlisle and was educated at Queen's College, Oxford where he was a fellow from 1710 to 1726. It is said he was befriended by Joseph Addison initially because of a poem he wrote called "Rosamond" which Addison admired greatly.

In 1717, when Addison became Secretary of State, he made Tickell Under-Secretary. From 1725 he was Secretary to the Lords Justices of Ireland.

He contributed pieces to "The Spectator" and "The Guardian", and was involved in a great literary controversy when his translation of Book 1 of "The Iliad" came out in 1715. The argument arose because Alexander Pope, who had just translated the same work, lambasted Addison claiming that he had done the work to overshadow Pope. Addison probably did correct the manuscript but the work was undoubtedly Tickell's.

Other of Tickells's works are "Kensington Gardens" and "Colin and Lucy".

Trevor-Roper, Hugh Redwald Born 1914

One of the greatest modern historians, Hugh Trevor-Roper was born in the tiny Northumberland village of Glanton. His education took place at Charterhouse and Oxford to the latter of which he returned in 1957 as Regius Professor of Modern History.

He is best-known for his book, "The Last Days of Hitler" which he wrote in 1947 after his wartime job in British Intelligence, but his main field of study ranges from the mid 16th to the late 17th century.

Wallas, Graham   1858 - 1932

A product of Shrewsbury School and Oxford's Corpus Christi, Graham Wallas, yet again the son of a clergyman, was born in

Sunderland. He taught at Highgate until 1895 when he moved to the London School of Economics. In 1908 he became a member of the Senate of London University. In 1914 and until 1923 he was Professor of Political Science at the London School of Economics.

From 1886 to 1904 he was one of the organising members of the Fabian Society.

Of his books, "Men and Ideas", 1940, and "The Great Society" 1914 are the best-known.

Watson, Richard   1833-1891

Richard Watson was known as the Teesdale Poet or Bard. He was born in the village of Middleton-in-Teesdale in 1833, son of a lead-miner. Lead-mining was the principal occupation in the dale at that time. As a schoolboy the young Watson demonstrated unusual skill at essay-writing and poetry and he was taken under the wing of a local clergyman who gave him extra tuition at no fee. He left school at the age of ten, following the death of his father, and he had to become the man of the house.

He married, when he was 24, Nancy Brumwell from the Teesdale hamlet of Ettersgill.

He had already been composing poems for several years and found that other people liked his work. His first poem to appear in the widely-read newspaper, the Teesdale Mercury', was a conversation between a tower of barnard Castle and a new railway bridge. The poem was very well-received and Watson was soon in demand to read his work at concerts. He rarely received a fee for such engagements although he might have written a poem especially for the occasion.

His great ambition was to see his poems in print in a book and, since nobody was willing to finance such a venture, he paid to have it done himself. Five hundred copies of 'The Poetical Works of Richard Watson' were published and offered for sale at one shilling a copy. Watson managed to recover the cost of printing, but only just.

He often considered emigrating to Australia or Canada but he was too attached to Teesdale. He had a strange attitude to life and was a poor manager of money. If he had some in his pocket, then he stayed away from work until he needed more but so did many of his leadmining colleagues. Because of this fault, his wife and family also suffered. One of the most famous tales about Watson was that he procured a hank of wool so that his wife could knit him a scarf and when she consistently failed to do so he wore the hank of wool round his neck instead.

Wilson, Joe   1841 - 1875

Joe Wilson, a Geordie if ever there was one was born on 29th November, 1841. His father was a joiner and cabinet maker while his mother made straw bonnets. They lived in Newcastle. At fourteen he went to learn the trade of a printer but his hobby was writing songs. When he was only seventeen years old his first book was published. Four years later he set up in business as a printer himself and a year later had his first big success with "Wor Geordy's Account o' the Great Boat Race atwixt Chambers an' Green". Soon afterwards he published "Tyneside Sangs".

Not only was Joe a writer of songs he was also a singer and as a boy and a young man he sang in the choir at All Saints. We can rightly give Joe the title of "The Geordie Bard" for he wrote sentimental as well as comic songs and poems.

In his print shop Joe's twin brother inked the roller while Joe worked at composing and printing at the same time. Eventually he gave up printing and gave more and more time to professional entertainment. He was for a time the manager of a concert hall at Spennymoor. He travelled all over the country entertaining. In 1871 he became the landlord of the Adelaide Hotel in Newcastle's New Bridge Street. For a time things went well but a year later he gave up the job. He had been drinking too heavily but now he joined a Temperance Society and began to write songs and poems for the movement. He needed some means of support. He returned for a time to the printing trade. Then it was back to the entertainment business with songs and lantern slides. News that he was back on the boards soon spread and he was given many engagements. Illness then overtook him. He made his last appearance at the Royal Star Theatre in Stockton-on-Tees, a benefit concert in 1874. He had many friends and money was raised to help him through his illness. Unfortunately, on February 12th 1875 he died when only thirty-three years old and was buried in the old cemetery at Jesmond. His epitaph, taken from his own autobiography is most apt

"It's been me aim t' hev a place   Wi' writin bits o' hyemly sangs
I' th' hearts o' th' Tyneside people,   Aw think they'll sing."

Wordsworth, Christopher   1774 - 1846

This man was the youngest brother of the famous William and was, like him, born at Cockermouth in Cumberland. Like his brother he gained his early education at Hawkshead Grammar School and followed him to Cambridge University but Christopher went to Trinity College, not St. John's. In 1798 he became a Fellow of Trinity and took holy orders. His first parish was Ashby-with-Oby and Thirne in Norfolk. In 1808 he became Dean of Bocking in Essex before moving on to become rector of St. Mary's, Lambeth and in 1815 of Sundridge in Kent. By 1820, he was rector of Buxted-with-Uckfield in Sussex. In the same year he became Master of Trinity College, a post he was to hold for twenty-one years. 1817 had been the year in which he was appointed Chaplain to the House of Commons. As well as being Master of Trinity he also held the post of Vice-Chancellor of Cambridge University.

In 1810 he published an "Ecclesiastical Biography" a selection of 'lives'.

One of his sons, Charles, was tutor to the great Gladstone.

Wordsworth, William   1770 - 1850

Genius, philosopher, madman and bore are all terms which have been applied at some time to the best-known of the Lake poets, William Wordsworth.

He was born at Cockermouth in what was then Cumberland in April 1770, son of an attorney. When he was eight, he was sent to the grammar school at Hawkshead, which he was to attend for nine years. He was a tough and normal boy but one who was acutely aware of Nature. His father died when he was fourteen and three years later William went off to St. John's College, Cambridge for a four-year stay during which he studied little. He was awarded his degree in 1791 and spent four months unemployed in London. While in France on a visit, he fell in love with Annette Vallon who duly presented him with a daughter, Ann Caroline. Wordsworth had meanwhile become embroiled in French revolutionary politics, which may be why he fled back to England before even seeing his child. Although a month later Britain and France were at war, Wordsworth bravely travelled to Paris but failed to see Annette. The war continued for nine years. Wordsworth was left a legacy of £900 and with it he and his sister Dorothy leased a house in Dorset where he was often visited by the poet Coleridge. He forgot Annette and grew closer to his younger sister, Dorothy. Such an affection grew with Coleridge that the Wordsworths moved to Somerset to be near him. Just before Christmas in 1799 they moved to Dove Cottage at Grasmere in the Lake District and here William did his best work in the eight years he lived there. He composed his poetry in the open air and wrote it down later, but he detested the physical act of writing and underwent considerable physical distress when he had it to do. In 1802, Wordsworth and his sister visited Annette and their child in France.

On his return to England he married his cousin, Mary Hutchinson but Dorothy continued to live with them as Coleridge was derided more and more by her brother. In 1805 his young seafaring brother, John, died, and, almost as a direct consequence, Wordsworth became a fervent supporter of Christianity and the State, abandoning his questioning attitude and his republican sentiments.

In 1808, the family moved to Rydal Mount and Wordsworth grew progressively richer and more famous until his death there in 1850. In 1814 he had acquired the peculiar appointment as Distributor of Stamps for Cumberland and Westmorland for which he was paid £1,000 a year until 1842 when he gave it up. In 1843, he was made Poet Laureate and in 1845 met Queen Victoria.

He was buried in Grasmere churchyard.

Young,   Emily   Hilda   1880 - 1949

Born in Northumberland, Emily Young moved to Bristol after her marriage in 1902. Her novels are referred to as being of the school of

Jane Austen. In 1930 she was awarded the Tait Black Memorial Prize for her novel "Miss Mole".

Her writing found success in 1910 with "A Corn of Wheat" and continued until 1947 with "Chatterton Square".

EXTRACTS AND WORKS OF THE GREAT NORTHERN WRITERS

SHE WALKS IN BEAUTY

She walks in beauty, like the night
Of cloudless climes and starry skies,
And all that's best of dark and bright
Meet in her aspect and her eyes,
Thus mellow'd to that tender light
Which heaven to gaudy day denies.

One shade the more, one ray the less,
Had half impair'd the nameless grace
Which waves in every raven tress,
Or softly lightens o'er her face,
Where thoughts serenely sweet express
How pure, how dear their dwelling-place.

And on that cheek and o'er that brow
So soft, so calm, yet eloquent,
The smiles that win, the tints that glow
But tell of days in goodness pent,
A mind at peace with all below,
A heart whose love is innocent.
                              Lord Byron

NO MORE A-ROVING

So, we'll go no more a-roving
So late into the night,
Though the heart be still as loving,
And the moon be still as bright.

For the sword outwears its sheath,
And the soul outwears the breast,
And the heart must pause to breathe,
And love itself have rest.

Though the night was made for loving,
And the day returns too soon,
Yet we'll go no more a-roving
By the light of the moon.
                              Lord Byron

A SONNET "FROM THE PORTUGUESE"

I thought once how Theocritus had sung
Of the sweet years, the dear and wished-for years,
Who each one in a gracious hand appears

To bear a gift for mortals, old or young:
And, as I mused it in his antique tongue,
I saw, in gradual vision through my tears,
The sweet, sad years, the melancholy years,
Those of my own life, who by turns had flung
A shadow across me. Staightway I was 'ware,
So weeping, how a mystic Shape did move
Behind me, and drew me backward by the hair;
And a voice said in mastery, while I strove,...
"Guess now who holds thee?" — "Death," I said.
But there,
The silver answer rang..."Not Death, but Love."
                    Elizabeth Barrett Browning

THE CHILDREN'S CRY

Do ye hear the children weeping, O my brothers,
Ere the sorrow comes with years?
They are leaning their young heads against their mothers,
And that cannot stop their tears.
The young lambs are bleating in the meadows,
The young birds are chirping in the nest,
The young fawns are playing with the shadows,
The young flowers are blowing toward the west
But the young, young children, O my brothers,
They are weeping bittelry!
They are weeping in the playtime of the others,
In the country of the free.

"For oh," say the children, "we are weary
And we cannot run or leap;
If we cared for any meadows, it were merely
To drop down in them and sleep.
Our knees tremble sorely in the stooping,
We fall upon our faces trying to go
And underneath our heavy eyelids drooping
The reddest flower would look as pale as snow
For, all day, we drag our burden tiring
Through the coal-dark, undergound;
On all day, we drive the wheels of iron
In the factories, round and round.
"For all day the wheels are droning, turning;
Their wind comes in our faces,
Till our hearts turn, our heads with pulses burning,
And the walls turn in their places:
Turns the sky in the high window, blank and reeling,
Turns the long light that drops adown the wall,
Turn the black flies that crawl along the ceiling:

All are turning, all the day, and we with all.
And all day, the iron wheels are droning,
And sometimes we could pray,
'O ye wheels' (breaking out in a mad moaning)
'Stop! be silent for to-day!'"

Ay! be silent! Let them hear each other breathing
For a moment, mouth to mouth!
Let them touch each other's hands, in a fresh wreathing
Of their tender human youth!
Let them feel that this cold metallic motion
Is not all the life God fashions or reveals:
Let them prove their living souls against the notion
That they live in you, or under you, O wheels!
Still, all day, the iron wheels go onward
Grinding life down from its mark;
And the children's souls, which God is calling sunward,
Spin on blindly in the dark.
    Elizabeth Barrett Browning

EXTRACT FROM
"THE SWEETNESS OF ENGLAND"

...such an up and down
Of verdure, — nothing too much up or down,
A ripple of land, such little hills, the sky
Can stoop to tenderly and the wheatfields climb;
Such nooks of valleys lined with orchises,
Fed full of noises by invisible streams;
And open pastures where you scarcely tell
White daisies from white dew, — at intervals
The mythic oaks and elm-trees standing out
Self-poised upon their prodigy of shade, —
I thought my father's land was worthy too
Of being my Shakespeare's.

Breaking into voluble ecstasy
I flattered all the beauteous country round,
As poets use, the skies, the clouds, the fields,
The happy violets hiding from the roads
The primroses run down to, carrying gold;
The tangled hedgerows, where the cows push out
Impatient horns and tolerant churning mouths
'Twixt dripping ash-boughs, — hedgerows all alive
With birds and gnats and large white butterflies
Which look as if the May-flower had caught life
And palpitated forth upon the wind;
Hills, vales, woods, netted in a silver mist,

Farms, granges, doubled up among the hills;
And cattle grazing in the watered vales,
And cottage-chimneys smoking from the woods,
And cottage-gardens smelling everywhere,
Confused with smell of orchids.
                    Elizabeth Barrett Browning

A MUSICAL INSTRUMENT

What was he doing, the great god Pan,
Down in the reeds by the river?
Spreading ruin and scattering ban,
Splashing and paddling with hoofs of a goat,
And breaking the golden lilies afloat
With the dragon-fly on the river.

He tore out a reed, the great god Pan,
From the deep cool bed of the river:
The limpid water turbidly ran,
And the broken lilies a-dying lay,
And the dragon-fly had fled away,
Ere he brought it out of the river.

High on the shore sate the great god Pan,
While turbidly flowed the river;
And hacked and hewed as a great god can,
With his hard bleak steel at the patient reed,
Till there was not a sign of a leaf indeed
To prove it fresh from the river.

He cut it short, did the great god Pan
(How tall it stood in the river!),
Then drew the pith, like the heart of a man,
Steadily from the outside ring,
And notched the poor dry empty thing
In holes, as he sate by the river.
                    Elizabeth Barrett Browning

EXTRACT FROM "THE RUINED COTTAGE"

Ay, Charles! I knew that this would fix thine eye;...
This woodbine wreathing round the broken porch,
Its leaves just withering, yet one autumn flower
Still fresh and fragrant; and yon hollyhock
That through the creeping weeds and nettles tall
Peers taller, lifting, column-like, a stem
Bright with its roseate blossoms. I have seen

Many an old convent reverend in decay,
And many a time have trod the castle courts
And grass-green halls, yet never did they strike
Home to the heart such melancholy thoughts
As this poor cottage. Look! its little hatch
Fleeced with that grey and wintry moss; the roof
Part moulder'd in, the rest o'ergrown with weeds,
House-leek, and long thin grass, and greener moss;
So Nature steals on all the works of man,
Sure conqueror she, reclaiming to herself
His perishable piles.
I led thee here,
Charles, not without design; for it hath been
My favourite walk even since I was a boy;
And I remember, Charles, this ruin here,
The neatest confortable dwelling-place!
That when I read in those dear books which first
Woke in my heart the love of poesy,
How with the villagers Erminia dwelt,
And Calidore for a fair shepherdess
Forsook his quest to learn the shepherd's lore,
My fancy drew from this the little hut
Where that poor princess wept her hopeless love,
Or where the gentle Calidore at eve
Led Pastorella home.
Robert Southey

EXTRACTS FROM THE JOURNAL OF DOROTHY WORDSWORTH

When we were in the woods beyond Gowbarrow Park we saw a few daffodils close to the water-side. We fancied that the lake had floated the seeds ashore, and that the little colony had so sprung up. But as we went along there were more and yet more; and at last, under the boughs of the trees, we saw that there was a long belt of them along the shore, about the breadth of a country turnpike road. I never saw daffodils so beautiful. They grew among the mossy stones about and about them; some rested their heads upon these stones, as on a pillow, for weariness; and the rest tossed and reeled and danced, and seemed as if they verily laughed with the wind, that blew upon them over the lake; they looked so gay, ever glancing, ever changing. This wind blew directly over the lake to them. There was here and there a little knot, and a few stragglers higher up; but they were so few as not to disturb the simplicity, unity, and life of that one busy highway. We rested again and again.
Dorothy Wordsworth

EXTRACTS FROM THE GRASMERE JOURNAL

MAY 14TH, 1800 (WEDNESDAY). Wm. and John set off into Yorkshire after dinner at ½ past 2 o'clock, cold pork in their pockets. I left them at the turning of the Lowwood bay under the trees. My heart was so full that I could hardly speak to W. when I gave him a farewell kiss. I sate a long time upon a stone at the margin of the lake, and after a flood of tears my heart was easier. The lake looked to me, I knew not why, dull and melancholy, and the weltering on the shores seemed a heavy sound. I walked as long as I could amongst the stones of the shore. The wood rich in flowers; a beautiful yellow, palish yellow, flower, that looked thick, round, and double, and smelt very sweet—I supposed it was a ranunculus. Crowfoot, the grassy-leaved rabbit-toothed white flower, strawberries, geranium, scentless violets, anemones two kinds, orchises, primroses. The heckberry very beautiful, the crab coming out as a low shrub. Met a blind man, driving a very large beautiful Bull, and a cow—he walked with two sticks. Came home by Clappersgate. The valley very green; many sweet views up to Rydalehead, when I could juggle away the fine houses; but they disturbed me, even more than when I have been happier; one beautiful view of the Bridge, without Sir Michael's. Sate down very often, though it was cold. I resolved to write a journal of the time till W. and J. return, and I set about keeping my resolve, because I will not quarrel with myself, and because I shall give Wm. pleasure by it when he comes home again...

(MAY 16th,) FRIDAY MORNING. Warm and mild, after a fine night of rain. Transplanted radishes after breakfast, walked to Mr. Gell's with the books, gathered mosses and plants. The woods extremely beautiful with all autumnal variety and softness. I carried a basket for mosses, and gathered some wild plants. Oh! that we had a book of botany. All flowers now are gay and deliciously sweet. The primrose still pre-eminent among the later flowers of the spring. Foxgloves very tall, with their heads budding. I went forward round the lake at the foot of Loughrigg Fell. I was much amused with the business of a pair of stone-chats; their restless voices as they skimmed along the water following each other, their shadows under them, and their returning back to the stones on the shore, chirping with the same unwearied voice. Could not cross the water, so I went round by the stepping-stones. The morning clear but cloudy, that is the hills were not overhung by mists. After dinner Aggy weeded onions and carrots. I helped for a little—wrote to Mary Hutchinson—washed my head—worked. After tea went to Ambleside—a pleasant cool but not cold evening. Rydale was very beautiful, with spear-shaped streaks of

polished steel. No letters!—only one newspaper. I returned by Clappersgate. Grasmere was very solemn in the last glimpse of twilight; it calls home the heart to quietness. I had been very melancholy in my walk back. I had many of my saddest thoughts, and I could not keep the tears within me. But when I came to Grasmere I felt that it did me good...

(JULY) 27TH, SUNDAY. Very warm. Molly ill. John bathed in the lake. I wrote out RUTH in the afternoon. In the morning, I read Mr. Knight's LANDSCAPE. After tea we rowed down to Loughrigg Fell, visited the white foxglove, gathered wild strawberries, and walked up to view Rydale. We lay a long time looking at the lake; the shores all embrowned with the scorching sun. The ferns were turning yellow, that is, here and there one was quite turned. We walked round by Benson's wood home. The lake was now most still, and reflected the beautiful yellow and blue and purple and grey colours of the sky. We heard a strange sound in the Bainriggs wood, as we were floating on the water; it seemed in the wood, but it must have been above it, for presently we saw a raven very high above us. It called out, and the dome of the sky seemed to echo the sound. It called again and again as it flew onwards, and the mountains gave back the sound, seeming as if from their centre; a musical bell-like answering to the bird's hoarse voice. We heard both the call of the bird, and the echo, after we could see him no longer. We walked up to the top of the hill again in view of Rydale—met Mr. and Miss Simpson on horseback. The crescent moon which had shone upon the water was now gone down. Returned to supper at 10 o'clock.

(OCTOBER) 11TH, SATURDAY. A fine October morning. Sat in the house working all the morning. William composing. Sa' Ashburner learning to mark. After dinner we walked up Greenhead Gill in search of a sheepfold. We went by Mr. Olliff's, and through his woods. It was a delightful day, and the views looked excessively cheerful and beautiful, chiefly that from Mr. Olliff's field, where our house is to be built. The colours of the mountains soft and rich, with orange fern; the cattle pasturing upon the hill-tops; kites sailing in the sky above our heads; sheep bleating and in lines and chains and patterns scattered over the mountains. They come down and feed on the little green islands in the beds of the torrents, and so may be swept away. The sheepfold is falling away. It is built nearly in the form of a heart unequally divided. Look down the brook, and see the drops rise upwards and sparkle in the air at the little falls, the higher sparkles the tallest. We walked along the turf of the mountain till we came to a cattle track, made by the cattle which come upon the hills. We drank tea at Mr. Simpson's, returned at about nine—a fine mild night.

(NOVEMBER) 24TH, (1801) TUESDAY. A rainy morning. We all were well except that my head ached a little, and I took my breakfast in bed. I read a little of Chaucer, prepared the goose for dinner, and then we all walked out. I was obliged to return for my fur tippet and spencer, it was so cold. We had intended going to Easedale, but we shaped our course to Mr. Gell's cottage. It was very windy, and we heard the wind everywhere about us as we went along the lane, but the walls sheltered us. John Green's house looked pretty under Silver How. As we were going along we were stopped at once, at the distance perhaps of 50 yards from our favourite birch tree. It was yielding to the gusty wind with all its tender twigs, the sun shone upon it, and it glanced in the wind like a flying sunshiny shower. It was a tree in shape, with stem and branches, but it was like a Spirit of water. The sun went in, and it resumed its purplish appearance, the twigs still yielding to the wind, but not so visibly to us. The other birch trees that were near it looked bright and chearful, but it was a creature by its own self among them. We could not get into Mr. Gell's grounds — the old tree fallen from its undue exaltation above the gate. A shower came on when we were at Benson's. We went through the wood — it became fair. There was a rainbow which spanned the lake from the island-house to the foot of Bainriggs. The village looked populous and beautiful. Catkins are coming out; palm trees budding; the alder, with its plumb-coloured buds. We came home over the stepping-stones. The lake was foamy with white waves. I saw a solitary butter-flower in the wood. I found it not easy to get over the stepping sones. Reached home at dinner tme. Sent Peggy Ashburner somne goose. She sent me some honey, with a thousand thanks. "Alas! the gratitude of men has," etc. I went in to set her right about this, and sate a while with her. She talked about Thomas's having sold his land. "Ay," says she "I said many a time he's not come fra London to buy ou land, however." Then she told me with what pains and industry they had made up their taxes, interest, etc. etc., how they all got up at 5 o'clock in the morning to spin and Thomas carded, and that they had paid off a hundred pounds in the interest. She said she used to take such pleasure in the cattle and sheep. "O how pleased I used to be when they fetched them down, and when I had been a bit poorly I would gang out upon a hill and look ower 't fields and see them, and it used to do me so much good you cannot think." Molly said to me when I came in, "Poor body! she's very ill, but one does not know how long she may last. Many a fair face may gang before her." We sate by the fire without work for some time, then Mary read a poem of Daniel upon Learning. After tea Wm. read Spenser, now and then a little aloud to us. We were making his waistcoat. We had a note from Mrs. C., with bad news from poor C. — very ill. William went to John's

Grove. I went to meet him. Moonlight, but it rained. I met him before I had got as far as John Baty's—he had been surprised and terrified by a sudden rushing of winds, which seemed to bring earth sky and lake together, as if the whole were going to enclose him in; he was glad he was in a high road.

In speaking of our walk on Sunday evening, the 22nd November, I forgot to notice one most impressive sight. It was the moon and the moonlight seen through hurrying driving clouds immediately behind the Stone-Man upon the top of the hill on the Forest Side. Every tooth and every edge of rock was visible, and the Man stood like a Giant watching from the roof of a lofty caste. The hill seemed perpendicular from the darkness below it. It was a sight that I could call to mind at any time, it was so distinct.

(DECEMBER) 12TH, SATURDAY. A fine frosty morning—Snow upon the ground. I made bread and pies. We walked with Mrs. Luff to Rydale and came home the other side of the Lake, met Townley with his dogs. All looked chearful and bright. Helm Crag rose very bold and craggy, a Being by itself, and behind it was the large ridge of mountain, smooth as marble and snow white. All the mountains looked like solid stone, on our left, going from Grasmere, i.e. White Moss and Nab Scar. The snow hid all the grass, and all signs of vegetation, and the rocks showed themselves boldly everywhere, and seemed more stony than rock or stone. The birches on the crags beautiful, red brown and glittering. The ashes glittering spears with their upright stems. The hips very beautiful, and so good!! and, dear Coleridge! I ate twenty for thee, when I was by myself. I came home first—they walked too slow for me. Wm. went to look at Langdale Pikes. We had a sweet invigorating walk. Mr. Clarkson came in before tea. We played at cards—sate up late. The moon shone upon the water below Silver—How, and above it hung, combining with Silver-How on one side, a bowl-shaped moon, the curve downwards; the white fields, glittering roof of Thomas Ashburner's house, the dark yew tree, the white fields gay and beautiful. Wm. lay with his curtains open that he might see it.

JANUARY 30TH, (1802) SATURDAY. A cold dark morning. William chopped wood—I brought it in a basket. A cold wind. Wm. slept better, but he thinks he looks ill—he is shaving now. He asks me to set down the story of Barbara Wilkinson's turtle dove. Barbara is an old maid. She had two turtle doves. One of them died, the first year I think. The other bird continued to live alone in its cage for 9 years, but for one whole year it had a companion and daily visitor—a little mouse, that used to come and feed with it; and the dove would caress it, and cower over it with its wings, and make a

loving noise to it. The mouse, though it did not testify equal delight in the dove's company, yet it was at perfect ease. The poor mouse disappeared, and the dove was left solitary till its death. It died of a short sickness, and was buried under a tree with funeral ceremony by Barbara and her maidens, and one or two others....
Dorothy Wordsworth

EXTRACT FROM THE JOURNAL OF DOROTHY WORDSWORTH

Friday, 14th May—A very cold morning—hail and snow showers all day. We went to Brothers wood, intending to get plants, and to go along the shore of the lake to the foot. We did go a part of the way, but there was no pleasure in stepping along that difficult sauntering road in this ungenial weather. We turned again, and walked backwards and forwards in Brothers wood. William tired himself with seeking an epithet for the cuckoo. I sate a while upon my last summer seat, the mossy stone. William's unemployed, beside me, and the space between, where Coleridge has so often lain. The oak trees are just putting forth yellow knots of leaves. The ashes with their flowers passing away, and leaves coming out; marsh marigolds in full glory; the little star plant, a star without a flower. We took home a great load of gowans, and planted them about the orchard. After dinner, I worked bread, then came and mended stockings beside William; he fell asleep.

After tea I walked to Rydale for letters. It was a strange night. The hills were covered over with a slight covering of hail or snow, just so as to give them a hoary winter look with the black rocks. The woods looked miserable, the coppices green as grass, which looked quite unnatural, and they seemed half shrivelled up, as if they shrank from the air. O, thought I! what a beautiful thing God has made winter to be, by stripping the trees, and letting us see their shapes and forms. What a freedom does it seem to give to the storms! There were several new flowers out, but I had no pleasure in looking at them. I walked as fast as I could back again with my letter from S.H. ... Met William at the top of White Moss....Near ten when we came in. William and Molly had dug the ground and planted potatoes in my absence. We wrote to Coleridge; sent off bread and frocks to the C's. Went to bed at half past eleven. William very nervous. After he was in bed, haunted with altering The Rainbow.
Dorothy Wordsworth

THE DAFFODILS

I wandered lonely as a cloud
That floats on high o'er vales and hills,
When all at once I saw a crowd,
A host, of golden daffodils;
Beside the lake, beneath the trees,
Fluttering and dancing in the breeze.

Continuous as the stars that shine
And twinkle on the milky way,
They stretched in never-ending line
Along the margin of a bay;
Ten thousand saw I at a glance,
Tossing their heads in sprightly dance.
The waves beside them danced; but they
Out-did the sparkling waves in glee:
A poet could not but be gay,
In such a jocund company:
I gazed—and gazed— but little thought
What wealth the show to me had brought:

For oft, when on my couch I le
In vacant or in pensive mood,
They flash upon the inward eye
Which is the bliss of solitude;
And then my heart with pleasure fills,
And dances with the daffodils
                    William Wordsworth

'PEACE BY ULLSWATER'
EXTRACT FROM "AIREY FORCE VALLEY"

...Not a breath of air
Ruffles the bosom of this leafy glen.
From the brook's margin, wide around, the trees
Are steadfast as the rocks; the brook itself,
Old as the hills that feed it from afar,
Doth rather deepen than disturb the calm
Where all things else are still and motionless
And yet, even now, a little breeze perchance
Escaped from boisterous winds that raged without
Has entered, by the sturdy oaks unfelt,
But in its gentle touch how sensitive
Is the light ash! that, pendent from the brow
Of yon dim cave, in seeming silence makes
A soft eye-music of slow-waving boughs,
Powerful almost as vocal harmony
To stay the wanderer's steps and soothe his thoughts.
                    William Wordsworth

FIDELITY

A barking sound the shepherd hears,
A cry as of a dog or fox;
He halts—and searches with his eyes
Among the scattered rocks:
And now at a distance can discern
A stirring in a brake of fern;
And instantly a dog is seen,
Glancing through that covert green.

The dog is not of mountain breed;
Its motions, too, are wild and shy;
With something, as the shepherd thinks,
Unusual in its cry.
It was a cove, a huge recess,
That keeps till June December's snow;
A lofty precipice in front,
A silent tarn below.
Far in the bosom of Helvellyn,
Remote from public road or dwelling.

Not free from boding thoughts, a while
The shepherd stood; then makes his way
O'er rocks and stones, following the dog
As quickly as he may;
Nor far had gone before he found
A human skeleton on the ground;
The appalled discoverer with a sigh
Looks round, to learn the history.

From those abrupt and perilous rocks
The man had fallen, that place of fear!
At length upon the shepherd's mind
It breaks, and all is clear:
He instantly recalled the name,
And who he was, and whence he came;
Remembered, too, the very day
On which the traveller passed this way.

But hear a wonder, for whose sake
This lamentable tale I tell!
The dog, which still was hovering nigh,
Repeating the same timid cry,
This dog had been through three months' space
A dweller in that savage place.
Yes, proof was plain that, since the day
When this ill-fated traveller died,
The dog had watched about the spot,
Or by his master's side.

William Wordsworth

'STORM OVER LANGDALE'
EXTRACT FROM "THE EXCURSION"

While at our pastoral banquet thus are sate
Fronting the window of that little cell,
I could not, ever and anon, forbear,
To glance an upward look on two huge Peaks,
That from some other vale peered into this,
"Those lusty twins," exclaimed our host, "if here
It were your lot to dwell, would soon become
Your prized companions. Many are the notes
Which, in his tuneful course, the wind draws forth
From rocks, woods caverns, heaths, and dashing shores;
And well those lofty brethren bear their part
In the wild concert—chiefly when the storm
Rides high; then all the upper air they fill
With roaring sound, that ceases not to flow,
Like smoke, along the level of the blast,
In mighty current; theirs, too, is the song
Of stream and headlong flood that seldom fails;
And, in the grim and breathless hour of noon,
Methinks that I have heard them echo back
The thunder's greeting. Nor have nature's laws
Left them ungifted with a power to yield
Music of finer tone; a harmony,
So do I call it, though it be the hand
Of silence, though there be no voice;—the clouds,
The mist, the shadows, light of golden suns,
Motions of moonlight, all come thither—touch,
And I have an answer—thither come, and shape
A language not unwelcome to sick hearts
And idle spirits:—there the sun himself,
At the calm close of summer's longest day,
Rests his substantial orb;—between those heights
And on the top of either pinnacle,
More keenly than elsewhere in night's blue vault,
Sparkle the stars, as of their station proud.
     William Wordsworth

LINES WRITTEN IN EARLY SPRING
I heard a thousand blended notes,
While in a grove I sat reclined,
In that sweet mood when pleasant thoughts
Bring sad thought to the mind.

To her fair works did Nature link
The human soul that through me ran;
And much it grieved my heart to think
What man has made of man.

Through primrose tufts, in that green bower,
The periwinkle trailed its wreaths;
And 'tis my faith that every flower
Enjoys tha air it breathes.

The birds around me hopped and played,
Their thoughts I cannot measure:—
But the least motion which they made,
It seemed a thrill of pleasure.

The budding twigs spread out their fan,
To catch the breezy air;
And I must think, do all I can,
That there was pleasure there.

If this belief from heaven be sent,
If such be Nature's holy plan,
Have I not reason to lament
What man has made of man?
            William Wordsworth

EXTRACT FROM "THE HARBOURS OF ENGLAND"

We only are to be reproached, who familiar with the Atlantic, are yet ready to accept with faith, as types of sea, the small waves, en papillote, and perukelike puffs of farinaceous foam, which were the delight of Backhuysen and his compeers. If one could but arrest the connoisseurs in the fact of looking at them with belief, and, magically introducing the image of a true sea-wave, let roll it up to them through the room, - one massive fathom's height, and rood's breadth of brine, passing them by but once, - dividing, Red Sea-like, on right hand and left, - but at least settling close before their eyes, for once in inevitable truth, what a sea-wave really is; its green mountainous giddiness of wrath, its overwhelming crest - heavy as iron, fitful as flame, clashing against the sky in long cloven edge, - its furrowed flanks, all ghastly clear, deep in transparent death, but all laced across with lurid nets of spume, and tearing open into meshed interstices their churned veil of silver fury, showing still the calm grey abyss below; that has no fury and no voice, but is as a grave always open, which the green sighting mounds do but hide for an instant as they pass. Would they, shuddering back from this wave of the true, implacable sea, turn forthwith to the papillotes? It might be so. It is what we are all doing, more or less, continually.
            John Ruskin

EXTRACT FROM
"THE LAY OF THE LAST MINSTREL"

X11

They sate them down on a marble stone,
(A Scottish monarch slept below;)
Thus spoke the Monk, in solemn tone:
'I was not always a man of woe;
For Paynim countries I have trod,
And fought beneath the Cross of God:
Now, strange to my eyes thine arms appear,
And their iron clang sounds strange to my ear.

X111

'In these far climes it was my lot
To meet the wondrous Michael Scott;
A wizard, of such dreaded fame,
That when, in Salamanca's cave,
Him listed his magic wand to wave,
The bells would ring in Notre Dame!
Some of his skill he taught to me;
And, Warrior, I could say to thee
The words that cleft Eildon hills in three,
And bridled the Tweed with a curb of stone:
But to speak them were a deadly sin;
And for having but thought them my heart within,
A treble penance must be done.

X1V

'When Michael lay on his dying bed,
His conscience was awakened;
He bethought him of his sinful deed,
And he gave me a sign to come with speed:
I was in Spain when the morning rose,
But I stood by his bed ere evening close.
The words may not again be said,
That he spoke to me, on death-bed laid;
They would rend this Abbaye's massy nave,
And pile it in heaps above his grave.

XV

'I swore to bury his Mighty Book,
That never mortal might therein look;
And never to tell where it was hid,
Save at his Chief of Branksome's need:
And when that need was past and o'er,
Again the volume to restore.
I buried him on St. Michael's night,
When the bell toll'd one, and the moon was bright,
And I dug his chamber among the dead,

When the floor of the chancel was stained red,
That his patron's cross might over him wave,
And scare the fiends from the Wizard's grave.

XVI

'It was a night of woe and dread,
When Michael in the tomb I laid!
Strange sounds along the chancel pass'd,
The banners waved without a blast'—
—Still spoke the Monk, when the bell toll'd one!—
I tell you, that a braver man
That William of Deloraine, good at need,
Against a foe ne'er spurr'd a steed;
Yet somewhat was he chill'd with dread,
And his hair did bristle upon his head.

XVII

'Lo, Warrior! now, the Cross of Red
Points to the grave of the mighty dead;
Within it burns a wondrous light,
To chase the spirits that love the night:
That lamp shall burn unquenchably,
Until the eternal doom shall be.'—
Slow moved the Monk to the broad flag-stone,
Which the bloody Cross was traced upon
He pointed to a secret nook;
An iron bar the Warrior took;
And the Monk made a sign with his wither'd hand,
The grave's huge portal to expand.

XVIII

With beating heart to the task he went;
His sinewy frame o'er the grave-stone bent;
With bar of iron heaved amain,
Tiill the toil-drops fell from his brows, like rain.
It was by dint of passing strength,
That he moved the massy stone at length.
I would you had been there, to see
How the light broke forth so gloriously,
Stream'd upward to the chancel roof,
And through the galleries far aloof!
No earthly flame blazed e'er so bright:
It shone like heaven's own blessed light,
And, issuing from the tomb,
Show'd the Monk's cowl, and visage pale,
Danced on the dark-brow'd Warrior's mail
And kiss'd his waving plume.

XIX

Before their eyes the Wizard lay,
As if he had not been dead a day.

His hoary beard in silver roll'd,
He seem'd some seventy winters old;
A palmer's amice wrapp'd him round,
With a wrought Spanish baldric bound,
Like a pilgrim from beyond the sea:
His left hand held his Book of Might;
A silver cross was in his right;
The lamp was placed beside his knee:
High and majestic was his look,
At which the fellest fiends had shook,
And all unruffled was his face:
They trusted his soul had gotten grace.

XX

Often had William of Deloraine
Rode through the battle's bloody plain,
And trampled down the warriors slain,
And neither known remorse nor awe;
Yet now remorse and awe he own'd;
His breath came thick, his head swam round,
When this strange scene of death he saw,
Bewilder'd and unnerv'd he stood,
And the priest pray'd fervently and loud:
With eyes averted prayed he;
He might not endure the sight to see,
Of the man he had loved so brotherly.

XX1

And when the priest his death-prayer had pray'd,
Thus unto Deloraine he said:—
'Now, speed thee what thou hast to do,
Or, Warrior, we may dearly rue;
For those, thou may'st not look upon,
Are gathering fast round the yawning stone!'—
Then Deloraine, in teror, took
From the cold hand the Mighty Book,
With iron clasp'd, and with iron bound:
He thought, as he took it, the dead man frown'd;
But the glare of the sepulchral light,
Perchance, had dazzled the warrior's sight.

XX11

When the huge stone sunk o'er the tomb,
The night return'd in double gloom;
For the moon had gone down, and the stars were few;
And, as the Knight and Priest withdrew,
With wavering steps and dizzy brain,
They hardly might the postern gain.
'Tis said, as through the aisles they pass'd,
They heard strange noises on the blast;
And through the cloister-galleries small,

Which at mid-height thread the chancel wall,
Loud sobs, and laughter louder, ran,
And voices unlike the voice of man;
As if the fiends kept holiday,
Because these spells were brought to day.
I cannot tell how the truth may be;
I say the tale as 'twas said to me.

XXIII

'Now, hie thee hence,' the Father said,
'And when we are on death-bed laid,
O may our dear Ladye, and sweet St John,
Forgive our souls for the deed we have done!'
The Monk return'd him to his cell,
And many a prayer and penance sped;
When the convent met at the noontide beel—
The Monk of St Mary's aisle was dead!
Before the cross was the body laid,
With hands clasp'd fast, as if still he pray'd.

XXIV

The Knight breathed free in the morning wind,
And strove his hardihood to find:
He was glad when he pass'd the tombstones gray,
Which girdle round the fair Abbaye;
For the mystic Book, to his bosom prest,
Feld like a load upon his breast;
And his joints, with nerves of iron twined,
Shook, like the aspen leaves in wind.
Full fain was he when the dawn of day
Began to brighten Cheviot gray;
He joy'd to see the cheerful light,
And he said Ave Mary, as well as he might.

XXV

The sun had brighten'd Cheviot gray,
The sun had brighten'd the Carter's side;
And soon beneath the rising day
Smiled Branksome Towers and Teviot's tide.
    Sir Walter Scott

EXTRACTS FROM THE JOURNAL OF GERTRUDE BELL

  "RUMEILEH, FEBRUARY 22nd. We have left villages behind, and are now camped among Arabs, praise be to God!

"*FEBRUARY 27th. Rakkah — which is no less than the summer capital of Harun er Rashid. My two soldiers go back to Aleppo from here, and I send this letter with them. I've engaged an Arab to come with me on the next stretch to Der, and I shall take one soldier from Rakkah.*

"*MARCH 6th. Circesium. The road along this part of the Euphrates is, as Xenophon says, exceedingly boring. He does not put it quite that way, but we mean the same thing. We rode for six hours along an eternal flat, with absolutely nothing to look at except at intervals the water wheels by the river bank. I am following in the steps of two invaders, Cyrus and Julian, and what with Xenophon and Marcellinus Ammianus I have the way before me pretty well described. It is fortunated, for there is nothing on the map. I forgot to tell you that at Der I saw the Arabs swimming across the Euphrates on inflated skins, exactly like the Assyrian soldiers in the bas reliefs in the British Museum.*

"*MARCH 10th. I have stolen two soldiers, one from Der, and one from Abu Kemal. They don't really mind at all, and I shall write to their commanding officers to explain their absence. I had a lucky morning, and was able to clear up some knotty points about old irrigation canals. A good many mistakes have been made in the topography of these parts, since no one apparently has ridden over the ground.*

Gertrude Bell

INTRODUCTION TO THE POEMS OF EMILY BRONTË

It would not have been difficult to compile a volume out of the papers left by my sisters, had I, in making the selection, dismissed from my consideration the scruples and the wishes of those whose u.. .en thoughts these papers held. But this was impossible: an influence, stronger than could be exercised by any motive of expediency, necessarily regulated the selection. I have, then, culled from the mass only a little poem here and there. The whole makes but a tiny nosegay, and the colour and perfume of the flowers are not such as fit them for festal uses.

It has been already said that my sisters wrote much in childhood and girlhood. Usually, it seems a sort of injustice to expose in print the crude thoughts of the unripe mind, the rude efforts of the unpracitsed hand; yet I venture to give three little poems of my sister Emily's, written in her sixteenth year, because they illustrate a point in her character.

At that period she was sent to school. Her previous life, with the exception of a single half-year, had been passed in the absolute retirement of a village parsonage, amongst the hills bordering Yorkshire and Lancashire. The scenery of these hills is not grand—it is not romantic; it is scarcely striking. Long low moors, dark with heath, shut-in little valleys, where as stream waters, here and there, a fringe of stunted copes. Mills and scattered cottages chase romance from these valleys; it is only higher up, deep in amongst the ridges of the moors, that Imagination can find rest for the sole of her foot: and even if she finds it there, she must be a solitude-loving raven—no gentle dove. If she demand beauty to inspire her, she must bring it inborn: these moors are too stern to yield any product so delicate. The eye of the gazer must itself brim with a "purple light," intense enought to perpetuate the brief flower-flush of August on the heather, or the rare sunset-smile of June; out of his heart must well the freshness, that in latter spring and early summer brightens the backen, nurtures the moss, and cherishes the starry flowers that spangle for a few weeks the pasture of the moor-sheep. Unless that light and freshness are innate and self-sustained, the drear prospect of a Yorkshire moor will be found as varren of poetic as of agricultural interest: where the love of a wild nature is strong, the locality will perhaps be clung to with the more passionate constancy, because from the hill-lovers's self come half its charm.

My sister Emily loved the moors. Flowers brighter than the rose bloomed in the blackest of the heath for her; out of a sullen hollow in a livid hill-side her mind could make an Eden. She found in the bleak solitude many and dear delights; and not the least and best beloved was—liberty.

Liberty was the breath of Emily's nostrils; without it, she perished. The change from her own home to a school, and from her own very noiseless, very secluded, but unrestricted an inartificial mode of life, to one of disciplined routine (though under the kindliest auspices), was what she failed in enduring. Her nature proved here too strong for her fortitude. Every morning when she woke, the vision of home and the moors rushed on her, and darkened and saddened the day that lay before her. Nobody knew what ailed her but me—I knew only too well. In this struggle her health was quickly broken: her white face, attenuated form, and failing strength, threatened rapid decline. I felt in my heart she would die, if she did not go home, and with this conviction obtained her recall. She had only been three months at school, and it was some years before the experiment of sending her from home was again ventured on. After the age of twenty, having meantime studied alone with diligence and perseverance, she went with me to an establishment on the Continent: the same suffering and conflict ensued, heightened by the strong recoil of her upright, heretic and English spirit from the gentle Jesuitry of the foreign and

Romish system. Once more she seemed sinking, but this time she rallied through the mere force of resolution: with inward remorse and shame she looked back on her former failure, and resolved to conquer in this second ordeal. She did conquer; but the victory cost her dear. She was never happy till she carried her hard-won knowledge back to the remote English village, the old parsonage house, and desolate Yorkshire hills. A very few years more, and she looked her last on those hills, and breathed her last in that house, and under the aisle of that obscure village church found her last lowly resting-place. Merciful was the decree that spared her when she was a stranger in a strange land, and guarded her dying bed with kindred love and congenial constancy.

Charlotte Brontë

THE FOLLOWING POEM WAS WRITTEN BY EMILY BRONTË WHILE AWAY AT SCHOOL, AGED 16

A little while, a little while,
The weary task is put away,
And I can sing and I can smile,
Alike, while I have holiday.

Where wilt thou go, my harassed heart—
What thought, what scene invites thee now?
What spot, or near or far apart,
Has rest for thee, my weary brow?

There is a spot 'mid barren hills,
Where winter howls, and driving rain;
But, if the dreary tempest chills,
There is a light that warms again.

The house is old, the trees are bare,
Moonless above bends twilight's dome;
But what on earth is half so dear—
So longed for—as the hearth of home?

The mute bird sitting on the stone,
The dank moss dripping from the wall,
The thorn-tree gaunt, the walks o'ergrown,
I love them—how I love them all!

Still, as I mused, the naked room,
The alien firelight died away;
And from the midst of cheerless gloom,
I passed to bright, unclouded day.

*A little and a lone green lane
That opened on a common wide;
A distant, dreamy, dim blue chain
Of mountains circling every side.*

*A heaven so clear, an earth so calm,
So sweet, so soft, so hushed an air;
And, deepening still the dream-like charm,
Wild moor-sheep feeding everywhere.*

*That was the scene, I knew it well;
I knew the turfy pathway's sweep,
That, winding o'er each billowy swell,
Marked out the tracks of wandering sheep.*

*Could I have lingered but an hour,
It well had paid a week of toil;
But Truth has banished Fancy's power;
Restraint and heavy task recoil.*

*Even as I stood with raptured eye,
Absorbed in bliss so deep and dear,
My hour of rest had fleeted by,
And back came labour, bondage, care.*
                    Emily Brontë

THE OLD STOIC

*Riches I hold in light esteem,
And Love I laugh to scorn;
And lust of fame was but a dream,
That vanished with the morn:*

*And if I pray, the only prayer
That moves my lips for me
Is, "Leave the heart that now I bear,
And give me liberty!"*

*Yes, as my swift days near their goal,
'Tis all that I implore;
In life and death a chainless soul,
With courage to endure.*
                    Emily Bronte

EXTRACT FROM WUTHERING HEIGHTS
(THE LAST THREE PARAGRAPHS)

My walk home was lengthened by a diversion in the direction of the kirk. When beneath its walls, I perceived decay had made progress, even in seven months: many a window showed black gaps deprived of glass; and slates jutted off, here and there, beyond the right line of the roof, to be gradually worked off in coming autumn storms.

I sought, and soon discovered, the three headstones on the slope next the moor: the middle one grey, and half buried in heath: Edgar Linton's only harmonised by the turf and moss creeping up its foot: Heathcliff's still bare.

I lingered round them, under that benign sky; watched the moths fluttering among the heath and harebells, listened to the soft wind breathing through the grass, and wondered how any one could ever imagine unquiet slumbers for the sleepers in that quiet earth.

Emily Brontë

NO COWARD SOUL

No coward soul is mine,
No trembler in the world's storm-troubled sphere:
I see Heaven's glories shine,
And Faith shines equal, arming me from Fear.

O God with my breast,
Almighty, ever-present Deity!
Life, that in me hast rest
As I, undying L_ _, have power in Thee!

Vain are the thousand creeds
That move men's hearts: unutterably vain;
Worthless as withered weeds,
Or idlest froth amid the boundless main,

To waken doubt in one
Holding so fast by Thy infinity,
So surely anchored on
The steadfast rock of Immortality.

With wide-embracing love
Thy Spirit animates eternal years,
Pervades and broods above,
Changes, sustains, dissolves, creates, and rears.

Though earth and moon were gone,
And suns and universes ceased to be,
And Thou wert left alone,
Every existence would exist in Thee.

There is not room for Death,
Nor atom that his might could render void:
Since Thou art Being and Breath
And what Thou art may never be destroyed.
                    Emily Brontë

IN MEMORY OF A HAPPY DAY IN FEBRUARY
(BEGUN IN FEBRUARY FINISHED NOVEMBER 10th 1842)

Blessed be Thou for all the joy
My soul has felt today!
O let its memory stay with me
And never pass away!

I was alone, for those I loved
Were far away from me,
The sun shone on the withered grass,
The wind blew fresh and free.

Was it the smile of early spring
That made my bosom glow?
'Twas sweet, but neither sun nor wind
Could raise my spirit so.

Was it some feeling of delight,
All vague and undefined?
No, 'twas a rapture deep and strong,
Expanding in my mind!

Was it a sanguine view of life
And all its transient bliss —
A hope of bright prosperity?
O no, it was not this!

It was a glimpse of truths divine
Unto my spirit given
Illumined by a ray of light
That shone direct from Heaven!

I knew there was a God on high
By whom all things were made.
I saw his wisdom and his power
In all his works displayed.

*But most throughout the moral world
I saw his glory shine;
I saw his wisdom infinite,
His mercy all divine.*

*Deep secrets of his providence
In darkness long concealed
Were brought to my delighted eyes
And graciously revealed.*

*And while I wondered and adored
His wisdom so divine,
I did not tremble at his power,
I felt that God was mine.*

*I knew that my Redeemer lived,
I did not fear to die;
I felt that I should rise again
To immortality.*

*I longed to view that bliss divine
Which eye hath never seen,
To see the glories of his face
Without the veil between.*
                          Anne Brontë

EXTRACT FROM "VILLETTE"

*And now the three years are past: M. Emanuel's return is fixed. It is Autumn; he is to be with me ere the mists of November come. My school flourishes, my house is ready: I have made him a little library, filled its shelves with books he left in my care: I have cultivated out of love for him (I was naturally no floris_ the plants he preferred, and some of them are yet in bloom. I thought I loved him when he went away: I love him now in another degree; he is more my own.
The sun passes the equinox; the days shorten, the leaves grow sere; but - he is coming.
Frosts appear at night; November has sent his fogs in advance; the wind takes its Autumn moan; but - he is coming. The skies hang full and dark - a rack sails from the west; the clouds cast themselves into strange forms - arches and broad radiations; there rise resplendent mornings - glorious, royal, purple as monarch in his state; the heavens are one flame; so wild are they, they rival battle at its thickest - so bloody, they shame Victory in her pride. I know some signs of the sky; I have noted them ever since childhood. God, watch that sail! Oh! guard it! The wind shifts to the west. Peace, peace, Banshee - 'keening' at every window! It will rise - it will swell*

- it shrieks out long: wander as I may through the house this night, I cannot lull the blast. The advancing hours make it strong: by midnight, all sleepless watchers hear and fear a wild south-west storm.
That storm roared frenzied for seven days. It did not cease till the Atlantic was strewn with wrecks: it did not lull till the deeps had gorged their full of sustenance. Not till the destroying angel of tempest had achieved his perfect work, would he fold the wings whose waft was thunder - the remor of whose plumes was storm.
Charlotte Brontë

THE MARCH OF THE SUNDAY SCHOOLS

Mr. Helstone produced his watch. "Ten minutes to two," he announced aloud. "Time for all to fall into line. Come." he seized his shovel-hat and marched away. All rose and followed en masse.

The twelve hundred children were drawn up in three bodies of four hundred souls each; in the rear of each regiment was stationed a band; between every twenty there was an interval, wherein Helstone posted the teachers in pairs. To the van of the armies he summoned:

"Grace Boultby and Mary Sykes lead out Whinbury."

"Margaret Hall and Mary Ann Ainley conduct Nunnely."

"Caroline Helstone and Shirley Keeldar head Briarfield."

Then again he gave command:

"Mr. Donne to Whinbury; Mr. Sweeting to Nunnely; Mr. Malone to Briarfield."

And these gentlemen stepped up before the lady-generals.

The rectors passed to the full front; the parish clerks fell to the extreme rear. Helstone lifted his shovel-hat. On an instant out clashed the eight bells in the tower, loud swelled the sounding bands, flute spoke and clarion answered, deep rolled the drums, and away they marched.

Not on combat bent, nor of foemen in search, was this priest-led and woman-officered company, yet their music played martial tunes, and, to judge by the eyes and carriage os fome—Miss Keeldar for instance—these sounds awoke, if not a martial, yet a longing spirit. Old Helstone, turning by chance, looked into her face; and he laughed, and she laughed at him.

"There is no battle in prospect," he said; "our country does not want us to fight for it. No foe or tyrant is questioning or threatening our liberty. There is nothing to be done. We are only taking a walk. Keep your hands on the reins, captain, and slack the fire of that spirit. It is not wanted, the more's the pity."

"Take your own advice, doctor," was Shirley's response....

"We shall pass through Royd Lane, to reach Nunnely Common by a short cut," said Mr. Helstone.

And into the straits of Royd Lane, they accordingly defiled. It was very narrow—so narrow that only two could walk abreast without falling into the ditch which ran along each side. They had gained the middle of it, when excitement became obvious in the clerical commanders. Boultby's spectacles and Helstone's Rehoboam were agitated; the curates nudged each other; Mr. Hall turned to the ladies and smiled.

"What is the matter!" was the demand.

He pointed with his staff to the end of the lane before them. Lo and behold! another, an opposition procession was there entering, headed also by men in black, and followed, as they could now hear, by music.

"Is it our double?" asked Shirley, "our manifold wraith? Here is a card turned up."

"If you wanted a battle, you are likely to get one—at least of looks," whispered Caroline, laughing.

"They shall not pass us!" cried the curates unanimously; "we'll not give way!"

"Give way!" retorted Helstone sternly, turning round; "who talks of giving way? You, boys, mind what you are about. The ladies I know iwll be firm. I can trust them. There is not a churchwoman here but will stand her ground against these folks, for the honour of the Establishment.— What does Miss Keeldar say?"

"She asks what is it."

"The Dissenting and Methodist schools, the Baptists, Independents, and Wesleyans, joined in unholy alliance, and turning purposely into this lane with the intention of obstructing our march and driving us back."

"Bad manners!" said Shirley, " and I hate bad manners. Of course they must have a lesson."

"A lesson in politeness," suggested Mr. Hall, who was ever for peace, "not an example of rudeness."

Old Helstone moved on. Quickening his pace, he marched some yard in advance of his company. He had nearly reached the other sable leaders, when he who appeared to act as the hostile commander-in-chief—a large greasy man, with black hair combed flat on his forehead—called a halt. He drew forth a hymn-book, gave out a verse, set a tune, and they all struck up the most dolorous of canticle.

Helstone signed to his bands. They clashed out with all the power of brass. He desired them to play Rule Britannia! and ordered the children to join in vocally, which they did with enthusiastic spirit. The enemy was sung and stormed *down, his psalm quelled. As far as noise went, he was conquered.*

"Now, follow me!" exclaimed Helstone; "not at a run, but at a firm smart pace. Be steady, every child and woman of you. Keep together. Hold on by each other's skirts if necessary."

And he strode on with such a determined and deliberate gait, and was, besides, so well seconded by his scholars and teachers, who did exactly as he told them, neither running nor faltering, but marching with cool, solid impetus — the curates too being compelled to do the same, as they were between two fire, Helstone and Miss Keeldar, both of whom watched any deviation with lynx-eyed vigilance, and were ready, the one with his cane, the other with her parasol, to rebuke the slightest breach of orders, the least independent or irregular demonstration — that the body of Dissenters was first amazed, then alarmed, then borne down, and pressed back, and at last forced to turn and leave the outlet from Royd Lane free. Boultby suffered in the onslaught, but Helstone and Malone, between them, held him up, and brought him through the business, whole in limb, though sorely tried in wind.

The fat Dissenter who had given out the hymn was left sitting in the ditch....

About half-past three the procession turned back, and at four once more regained the starting-place. Long lines of benches were arranged in the close-shorn fields round the school.

There the children were seated, and huge baskets, covered up with white cloths, and great smoking tin vessels were brought out. Ere the distribution of good things commenced, a brief grace was pronounced by Mr. Hall, and sung by the children. Their young voices sounded melodious, even touching, in the open air. Large currant buns, and hot, well-sweetened tea were then administered in the proper spirit of liberality. No stinting was permitted, on that day at least; the rule for each child's allowance being that it was to have about twice as much as it could possibly eat, thus leaving a reserve to be carried home for such as age, sickness, or other impediment prevented from coming to the feast. Buns and beer circulated meantime, among the musicians and church-singers; afterwards the benches were removed and they were left to unbend their spirits in licensed play.

A bell summoned the teachers, patrons, and patronesses to the schoolroom. Miss Keeldar, Miss Helstone, and many other ladies were already there, glancing over the arrangement of the separate trays and tables. Most of the female servants of the neighborhood, together with the clerks', the singers', and the musicians' wives, had been pressed into the service of the day as waiters. Each vied with the other in smartness and daintiness of dress, and many handsome forms were seen among the younger ones. About half a score were cutting bread-and-butter, another half-score supplying hot water, brought from the coppers of the rector's kitchen. The profusion of flowers and evergreens, decorating the white walls, the show of silver teapots and bright porcelain on the tables, the active figures, blithe faces, gay dresses flitting about everywhere, formed altogether a refreshing and lively spectacle. Everybody talked, not very loudly, but merrily, and the canary-birds sung shrill in their high-hung cages.

Caroline as the rector's niece, took her place at one of the three first tables; Mrs. Boultby and Margaret Hall officiated at the others. At these tables the élite of the company were to be entertained, strict rules of equality not being more the fashion at Briarfield than elsewhere. Miss. Helstone removed her bonnet and scarf, that she might be less oppressed with the heat. Her long curls, falling on her neck, served almost in place of veil, and for the rest, her muslin dress was fashioned modestly as a nun's robe, enabling her thus to dispense with the encumbrance of a shawl.

The room was filling. Mr Hall had taken his post beside Caroline; as she rearranged the cups and spoons before her, she whispered to him in a low voice remarks on the events of the day. He looked a little grave about what had taken place in Royd Lane, and she tried to smile him out of his seriousness...

Caroline now looked round for Shirley. She saw the rainbow scarf and purple dress in the centre of a throng of ladies, all well known to herself, but all of the order whom she systematically avoided whenever avoidance was possible. Shyer at some moments than at others, she felt just now no courage at all to join this company. She could not, however, stand alone where all others went in pairs or parties. so she approached a group of her own scholars, great girls, or rather young women, who were standing watching some hundreds of the younger children playing at blind-man's buff.

Miss. Helstone knew these girls liked her, yet she was shy even with them out of school. They were not more in awe of her than she of them. She drew near them now, rather to find protection in their company than to patronize them with her presence. By some instinct they knew her weakness, and with natural politeness they respected it. Her knowledge commanded their esteem when she taught them; her gentless attracted their regard; and because she was what they considered wise and good when on duty, they kindly overlooked her evident timidity when off. They did not take advantage of it. They stood round her still, civil, friendly, receiving her slight smiles and rather hurried efforts to converse with a good feeling and good breeding—the last quality being the result of the first—which soon set her at her ease.

Mr Sam Wynne coming up, with great haste to insist on the elder girls joining in the game as well as the younger ones, Caroline was again left alone. She was meditating a quiet retreat to the house when....the sudden and joyous clash of the bells summoned all to the church.

Charlotte Brontë

THE MONTHS

January brings the snow,
Makes our feet and fingers glow.

February brings the rain,
Thaws the frozen lake again.

March brings breezes loud and shrill,
Stirs the dancing daffodil.

April brings the primrose sweet,
Scatters daisies at our feet.

May brings flocks of pretty lambs,
Skipping by their fleecy dams.

June brings tulips, lilies, roses,
Fills the children's hands with posies.

Hot July brings cooling showers,
Apricots and gillyflowers.

August brings the sheaves of corn,
Then the harvest home is borne.

Warm September brings the fruit,
Sportsmen then begin to shoot.

Fresh October brings the pheasant,
Then to gather nuts is pleasant.

Dull November brings the blast,
Then the leaves are whirling fast.

Chill December brings the sleet,
Blazing fires and Christmas treat.

Sara Coleridge

KUBLA KHAN

In Xanadu did Kubla Khan
A stately pleasure-dome decree:
Where Alph, the sacred river, ran
Through caverns measureless to man
Down to a sunless sea.
So twice five miles of fertile ground
With walls and towers were girdled round:
And there were gardens bright with sinuous rills
Where blossom'd many an incense-bearing tree;
And here were forests ancient as the hills,
Enfolding sunny spots of greenery.

But oh! that deep romantic chasm which slanted
Down the green hill athwart a cedarn cover!
A savage place! as holy and enchanted
As e'er beneath a waning moon was haunted
By woman wailing for her demon-lover!

And from this chasm, with ceaseless turmoil seething,
As if this earth in fast thick pants were breathing,
A mighty fountain momently was forced:
Amid whose swift half-intermitted burst
Huge fragments vaulted like rebounding hail:
Or chaffy grain beneath the thresher's flail:
And mid these dancing rocks at once and ever
It flung up momently the sacred river.
Five miles meandering with a mazy motion
Through wood and dale the sacred river ran,
Then reach'd the caverns measureless to man,
And sank in tumult to lifeless ocean:
And 'mid this tumult Kubla heard from far
Ancestral voices prophesying war!

The shadow of the dome of pleasure
Floated midway on the waves;
Where was heard the mingled measure
From the fountain and the caves.
It was a miracle of rare device
A sunny pleasure-dome with caves of ice!

A damsel with a dulcimer
In a vision once I saw:
It was an Abyssinian maid,
And on her dulcimer she play'd,
Singing of Mount Abora.
Could I revive within me
Her symphony and song,
To such a deep delight 'twould win me
That with music loud and long,
I would build that dome in air,

That sunny dome! those caves of ice!
And all who heard whould see them there,

And all should cry, Beward! Beware!
His flashing eyes, his floating hair!
Weave a circle round him thrice,
And close your eyes with holy dread,
For he on honey-dew hath fed,
And drunk the milk of Paradise.
     Samuel Taylor Coleridge

ANSWER TO A CHILD'S QUESTION

Do you ask what the birds say? The sparrow, the dove,
The linnet and thrush say, 'I love and I love!'
In the winter they're silent—the wind is so strong;
What it says, I don't know, but it sings a loud song.
But green leaves, and blossoms, and sunny warm weather,
And singing, and loving — all come back together.
But the lark is so brimful of gladness and love,
The green fields below him, the blue sky above,
That he sings, and he sings; and for ever sings he —
'I love my Love, and my Love love me!'
     Samuel Taylor Coleridge

'TOWN AND COUNTRY'
EXTRACT FROM "FROST AT MIDNIGHT."

For I was reared in the great city, pent 'mid cloisters dim,
And saw naught lovely but the sky and stars.
But thou, my Babe! shalt wander like a breeze
By lakes and sandy shores, beneath the crags
Of ancient mountain, and beneath the clouds,
Which image in their bulk both lakes and shores
And mountain crags: so shalt thou see and hear
The lovely shapes and sounds intelligible
Of that eternal language, which they God
Utters, who from eternity doth teach
Himself in all, and all things in himself.
Great universal Teacher! he shall mould
Thy spirit, and by giving make it ask.

Therefore all seasons shall be sweet to there,
Whether the summer clothe the general earth
With greenness, or the redbreast sit and sing
Betwixt the tufts of snow on the bare branch
Of mossy apple-tree, while the nigh thatch
Smokes in the sun-thaw; whether the eave-drops fall,
Heard only in the trances of the blast,
Or if the secret ministry of frost,
Shall hang them up in silent icicles,
Quietly shining to the quiet Moon.

Samuel Taylor Coleridge

FLANNAN ISLE

"Though three men dwell on Flannan Isle
To keep the lamp alight,
As we steered under the lee, we caught
No glimmer through the night."

A passing ship at dawn had brought
The news; and quickly we set sail,
To find out what strange thing might ail
The keepers of the deep-sea light.

The winter day broke blue and bright,
With glancing sun and glancing spray,
As o'er the swell our boat made way,
As gallant as a gull in flight.

But, as we neared the lonely Isle,
And looked up at the naked height,
And saw the lighthouse towering white,
With blinded lantern, that all night
Had never shot a spark
Of comfort through the dark,
So ghostly in the cold sunlight
It seemed that we were struck the while
With wonder all too dread for words.

And, as into the tiny creek
We stole beneath the hanging crag,
We saw three queer, black, ugly birds —
Too big by far, in my belief,
For cormorant or shag —
Like seamen sitting bolt-upright
Upon a half-tide reef:
But, as we neared, they plunged from sight,
Without a sound or spurt of white.

*And still too mazed to speak,
We landed, and made fast the boat,
And climbed the track in single file,
Each wishing he were safe afloat.
On any sea, however far,
So be it far from Flannan Isle:
And still we seemed to climb, and climb,
As though we'd lost all count of time,
And so must climb for evermore.
Yet, all too soon, we reached the door—
The black, sun-blistered lighthouse door,
That gaped for us ajar.*

*As, on the threshold, for a spell,
We paused we seemed to breathe the smell
Of limewash and of tar,
Familiar as our daily breath,
As though 'twere some strange scent of death:
And so, yet wondering, side by side
We stood a moment, still tongue-tied:
And each with black foreboding eyed
The door, ere we should fling it wide,
To leave the sunlight for the gloom:
Till, plucking courage up, at last,
Hard on each other's heels we passed
Into the living-room.*

*Yet, as we crowded through the door,
We only saw a table spread
For dinner, meat and cheese and bread;
But all untouched; and no one there:
As though, when they sat down to eat,
Ere they could ever taste,
Alarm had come; and they in haste
Had risen and left the bread and meat:
For at the table-head a chair
Lay tumbled on the floor.*

*We listened; but we only heard
The feeble cheeping of a bird
That starved upon its perch:
And, listening still, without a word,
We set about our hopeless search.*

*We hunted high, we hunted low,
And soon ransacked the empty house;
Then o'er the Island to and fro,
We ranged, to listen and to look
In every cranny, cleft, or nook
That might have hid a bird or mouse:
But though we searched from shore to shore,*

We found no sign in any place,
And soon again stood face to face
Before the gaping door,
And stole into the room once more
As frightened children steal.
Ay: though we hunted high and low,
And hunted everywhere,
Of the three men's fate we found no trace
Of any kind in any place,
But a door ajar, and an untouched meal
And an overtoppled chair.

And, as we listen'd in the gloom
Of that forsaken living-room —
A chill clutch on our breath —
We thought how ill-chance came to all
Who kept the Flannan Light:
And how the rock had been the death
Of many a likely lad:
How six had come to a sudden end,
And three had gone stark mad:
And one whom we'd all known as a friend
Had leapt from the lantern one still night,
And fallen dead by the lighthouse wall:
And long we thought
Of the three we sought,
And of what might yet befall.

Like curs a glance had brought to heel,
We listen'd, flinching there:
And look'd, and look'd, on the untouched meal
And the overtoppled chair.

We seemed to stand for an endless while,
Though still no word was said,
Three men alive on Flannan Isle,
Who thought on three men dead.
     Wilfrid Wilson Gibson

WEEL MAY THE KEEL ROW
As I came thro' Sandgate,
Thro' Sandgate, thro' Sandgate,
As I came thro' Sandgate,
I heard a lassie sing,
'O weel may the keel row,
The keel row, the keel row,
O weel may the keel row,
That my laddie's in.

O wha is like my Johnny,
Sae leish, sae blythe, sae bonny?
He's foremost among the mony
Keel lads o' coaly Tyne:
He'll set and row so tightly,
Or in the dance — so sprightly —
He'll cut and shuffle sightly;
'Tis true — were he not mine.
He wears a blue bonnet,
Blue bonnet, blue bonnet;
He wears a blue bonnet, —
And a dimple on his chin:
And weel may the keel row,
The keel row, the keel row,
And weel may the keel row,
That my laddie's in?
                    Anonymous (18th century)

EXTRACT FROM 'NATURE'
"THE PLEASURES OF IMAGINATION"

O ye dales
Of Tyne, and ye most ancient woodlands; where,
Oft as the giant flood obliquely strides,
And his banks open, and his lawns extend,
Stops short the pleased traveller to view,
Presiding o'er the scene, some rustic tower
Founded by Norman or by Saxon hands:
O ye Northumbrian shades, which overlook
The rocky pavement and the mossy falls
Of solitary Wensbeck's limpid stream;
How gladly I recall your well-known seats,
Beloved of old, and that delightful time
When, all alone, for many a summer's day,
I wandered through your calm recesses, led
In silence by some powerful hand unseen.
Nor will I e'er forget you; nor shall e'er
The graver task of manhood, or the advice
Of vulgar wisdom, move me to disclaim
Those studies which possessed me in the dawn
Of life, and fixed the colour of my mind
For every future year: whence even now
From sleep I rescue the clear hours of morn,
And, while the world around lies overwhelmed
In idle darkness, am alive to thoughts
Of honourable fame, of truth divine
Or moral, and of minds to virtue won
By the sweet magic of harmonious verse.
                    Mark Akenside

DARLINGTON FIFTY YEARS AGO

I stood on Bank Top when meadows were green,
Where little but Cuthbert's tall spire was seen -
With far in the distance, an old-fashioned shop,
And the old Town Hall, with its cupola top,
Where magnates arraign, and condemn those who sup
To regions below, - or rather lock-up.
No North-Eastern then had its trains to annoy
The dairyman's horse, or the passive ploughboy,
He would whistle away ne'er troubling his brain
About whistles that scream from the passenger train;
Victoria Road, and the streets that stand round,
In his path from the plough could never be found.
No Station, replete, with an Engineer's skill
Will e'er surpass that on Victoria Hill;
And the Park by the Skerne, with its walks and its ways,
Ne'er entered his mind in those slow going-days;
The Church of St. John's, with sweet sounding bells,
Stands now where the guide post told to Middleton Wells,
And Eastbourne so trim, with its dwellings and land,
Was the place where th ploughboy's courtship was plan'd;
Yes, that was the spot for sweet meadows and trees,
When soft breezes blew from the western leas,
No one then e'er dreamt of dwellings being reared,
Or that hedgerows and trees around should be cleared, -
That cowslips and violets should ever give way,
And be to the builders a spoil and a prey.
No Forge 'mid the fields, no smoke from the Hill,
Save that which arose from the old Priestgate Mill.
The serpentine Skerne roll'd its waters along
By Clay Row and Parkgate, in winter so strong,
But dwellers in houses ne'er felt once the worse.
As it spread over fields in its wild winter course,
For few could be seen where now crowded ones stand
By the banks of the Skerne and low lying land.
Now, tall smoking chimneys stand up everywhere,
With cloud-curling smoke high up in the air,
And the sparks from the Works, and hum from the Mills,
With pleasure and joy the workman's heart fills.
The Press, like a seed, lay slumbering and low,
Awaiting some power to give it a blow,
No Echo flashed out in its keen stirring way,
To light up the mind in this progressive day;
No North Star or Times gave news to the North,
(For light from the press had not glimmered forth).
No Central Hall, no learn'd Institute
To give to the town a Classic repute;
No Corporate Staff with a Mayor at its head,
Who by the Mace-bearer in dignity's led;
No honoured M.P., with grace and renown,

Then sat in the House, from this famed southern Town.
Now, treasures of knowledge in College and School
Are everywhere found to be the grand rule;
Fair maidens are train'd to enlighten this age,
And give it a lustre in history's page,
And the grand Grammar School, where learned Masters train
Aspiring youth, with rich food for the brain,
and a Library, free, where knowledge is stored
For an artizan's mind or the brain of a lord;
And places close by for true worship or prayer,
In this grand old Town are found everywhere;
'Twas here in days past, when through its lone vale,
The Passenger Coach ran first on the Rail,
A model for those in each country and clime
To raverse with speed through the boundries of time.

John Horsley

WOR GEORDY'S ALBUM
TEUN - "Pull Away Cheerily."

Here's wor Geordy's Album - he bowt it at Allan's,
That sells a' the beuks at the heed o' Dean Street,
An' what it contains me intenshun's te tell ye,
An' before aw conclude ye'll give in it's a treet:-
The forst it's wor Geordy wi' Peggy beside him,
They had them byeth teun when they got on the spree;
Then here's Bill King the Cobbler, that once wes a sowljor,
He's had his reet leg teun clean off be the knee.

Korus

So lissen, me lads, te what's i' Geordy's album,
Aw's sure it'll cause sum amusement the while,
For iv a' the queer mixtors o' foaksis an' fyeces,
Aw's sartin ye've nivor seen owt i' this style.

The next it's John Spencer, the famous eccentric,
That sells ivrything for a penny, that's true!
He can talk aboot owt, even nowt, that's a mazer,
An' argy on onything, ainshint or new;
Then here's Billy O'Rooke, - he's a regular cawshun,
Te scrape on the fiddle an' shoot a queer sang,
But he issent half daft tho he lucks awful silly,
When he puts oot a tung aboot half a yard lang.

The next i' the beuk's Jimmy Jonsin the Barber,
That shaves a' the foaks i' Darn Crook, an' cuts hair;
Then here's Davy Davis, the Newgate Street Preacher,
That tries all he can te spoil bettin men there;
Then here's Cameron the Jockey, belangin Newcassil,
A rider that few on the turf can excel;
The next's Jimmy Mooney, a Sweep throo the day-time,
But at neet he turns oot a real Grainger Street swell,

Here's a groop wi' Bob Chambers, an' Clasper, an' Cooper,
Three men that shud ivor be thowt on wi' pride;
An' here's game Jimmy Taylor, Jack Bright, an' Jim Percy,
Three promisin pullers, te keep up Tyneside;
The next is Tom Glenny, the clivor tragedian,
He's gain'd i' the aud an' new world greet renoon,
An' the reason aw think we shud think tha mair on him
He belangs like worsels to the canny aud town.

Then here's poor Ned Corvan, the comic Tynesider,
That myed the foaks laff till thor sides wes a' sair,
Wiv his humorous sangs; - an' the next's Geordy Ridley,
Another gud fellow, - but noo thor ne mair;
The next is me awn, that aw promised wor Peggy
Te fill up a page, an it's like me ye see, -
Thor issent ne mair, but the next time wor Geordy
Gets ony aw'll bring them an' show them te ye.

Joe Wilson

THE EPITAPH

Written at Edinburgh Infirmary
A Few Days Prior To His Death

"Ye lovers of the muse draw near,
And o'er this green grave drop a tear.
He named the "Teesdale Bard" lies here,
In death's domain.
Who'll tune your native lyre to cheer
Your hearts again."

"The beauties of his native Tees,
The rocks, and dells, and stately trees,
And cataracts grand; such scenes as these
His soul admired.
They were like sermons, and with ease
His muse inspired."

"A poor, hard-toiling, rustic bard,
His lot indeed was crooked and hard,
Of ease that wealth bestows, debarred,
A load of woes,
To suffering worth, 'tis the reward
This world bestows.

"But all his sorrows, cares, and woes,
Did here by death, come to a close,
His soul is now in sweet repose,
In endless rest,
Where none the least privation knows,
And all are blest."

Richard Watson

THE KING'S ENGLAND

There had not here as yet, Save cavern-shade, Aught been;
But this wide abyss Stood deep and dim,
Strange to its Lord, Idle and useless;
On which looked with his eyes The King firm of mind,
And beheld those places Void of joys;
Saw the dark cloud Lower in eternal night,
Swart under heaven, Dark and waste....
Here first shaped The Lord Eternal
Chief of all creatures, Heaven and Earth,
The firmament upreared, And this spacious land,
Established, By his strong powers, the Lord Almighty.
The Earth as yet was Not green with grass;
Ocean covered Swart in eternal night.

Caedmon